"Rivers" in Arizona

Stephen A. Bly

BACK TO THE BIBLE
LINCOLN, NE 68501

Copyright © 1991
by
Stephen A. Bly
All rights reserved.

2000 printed to date—1991
(5-7697—2M—41)
ISBN 0-8474-6624-8

Printed in the United States of America

CONTENTS

Testing the Waters 5
The Great Divide 19
Crashing In 35
Smooth Sailing 51
The Lucky Shirt 65
One of a Kind 79
Cruising 91
The Right Chemistry 103
Solid Gold 115
The Search 127

Testing the Waters

I told them to call and find out the right time. I mean, if the church service starts at 10:45, and we don't show up until 11:00, of course we will have to walk down in front of everyone, Jed Rivers muttered to himself as he scrunched down in his seat. He felt conspicuous in his six foot frame. He thought about his friends back in Ohio, Matt and T.J., who always hung out in the next to the last pew, right behind Mrs. Johnson and her hat.

I don't think ladies wear hats to church in Phoenix, he thought as a half smile escaped from his otherwise unflinching, square jaw. *But I'm sure not going to turn around and look. Last week the entire church in Ohio lined up to tell us good-bye. This week we don't know a person in the whole building. I'm glad You're here, Lord, or we'd be among total strangers.* Jed wasn't sure whether he was praying or just sighing.

During the last hymn he planned a quick exit. *I'll tell the folks I'm looking for a drinking fountain, hurry out to the entry, and then pile in the car and wait for them.*

The minute the service ended, Jed swung out into the aisle, but was clamped in place by a forceful hand on his shoulder. He turned around, seeing a man the size of a sumo wrestler grinning at him.

"Hello there. . . . You folks visiting today?" a voice boomed out of the grin.

Jed knew he was trapped. While his parents talked to the friendly greeter, the strong grip remained on his shoulder. Jed saw his sister, Catherine, scoot out the door toward the parking lot. Finally the big guy loosened his grip.

"Say, how old are you, son?"

With some apprehension Jed replied, "Er, 15. Why?"

"Well now, I would have guessed you to be a couple years older. As tall, and lean and strong as you are, I'd peg you for a basketball player. Say, my little Ginny is 15 too. You'll have to meet her." He shot a sudden glance around the emptying sanctuary, then called out to some folks visiting in the middle aisle.

"Margaret, have you seen little Ginny?"

Jed turned to see who was being addressed, and noticed that the lady responding was only slightly dwarfed by her husband. His mind momentarily slipped away from the sanctuary conversation to a couple of principles he had been developing in the past few years. *Rule #1—If you want to know what a girl's going to look like, look at her mom.* Oh, brother, Jed groaned, *this gal doesn't have a chance, except maybe as a linebacker for the Browns. Rule #2—If her dad has to hunt for people to introduce her, she must have zero personality.*

Jed breathed a sigh of relief when "little Ginny" could not be found. *Maybe we'll go visit a different church next week,* he hoped as they finally reached the car.

"Are you in a hurry to get home?" Mr. Rivers spoke to Catherine who slumped in the back seat.

She pulled her long, straight, brown hair over her eyes and hid behind it. "Yeah . . . to Ohio. I don't think I'm going to like Arizona," she moaned.

"But we've only been here three days," her mother encouraged.

"Yeah, but it was 105 degrees yesterday, and it's supposed to get hotter today. We start a new school tomorrow and I can't even find my clothes, let alone get them ready; and besides, I don't even know what kids wear to junior high out here. Why don't we just say we had a nice vacation and go back home?"

Mr. Rivers spoke up, "For starters, we sold our Ohio house, my job's out here, and we've just purchased a home here."

"Yeah, well, what other reasons do we have to stay?" Catherine pouted. She brushed her hair back, showing her brown eyes.

"Now, we all voted to move, remember?" her mom counseled.

"Yeah," Catherine continued, "but that was before I knew that Phoenix was halfway around the world from Ohio. I thought we were going to have a western adventure. There are a million people in Phoenix. A million people! And half of them were in that church! We might as well have moved to Chicago."

"Well, Jed," Mr. Rivers said, glancing to the back seat, "how did you like the church?"

"Oh, the church was all right. I suppose we'll get used to it. But I don't like having to sit up front."

"Well, I'm glad you liked it, Jed—because I told that friendly man who greeted us that you'd be at the youth meeting tonight."

"You what? The guy who eats a donut shop for breakfast?"

"Jed!" His mother's explosion kept him from continuing.

They spent the afternoon digging through boxes and trying to settle in a new house. Jed was about through with his pile when Catherine wandered in for an inspection.

Catherine stared at the bare walls. "What is this, Jed? No sports posters?"

Jed lay on his back in the middle of the room, bench pressing his barbells. "Yeah, well, we're a long way from Ohio State," he shrugged. "Have you seen my weight bench?"

"Weight bench? I can't even find my purple blouse. I guess you're going to have to root for Arizona State now." She dug through one of Jed's boxes.

"I don't know. How can you get excited about a team called the 'Sun Devils?' It sounds sort of un-Christian, you know."

"Oh. Well, I never thought 'Buckeyes' sounded all that spiritual. . . . Hey, where did you get this?" Catherine shrieked.

"What?"

"This picture of me in the bathtub at Grandma's."

"Oh, I don't know. . . . I think Mom packed most of that box. Probably out of her Memory Box or something. Let me see it."

"No way. There's no boy on earth, including a big brother, who's going to see me in the bathtub!"

"But you were just a baby, right?"

"Oh, sure. Then at some youth group activity they'll flash that up on the wall and I'll die."

"Are the junior high kids in the same group as high school?" Jed questioned.

"I don't know, but I'm not going tonight." Catherine clutched the picture and turned to go.

"Hey, how come? I've *got* to go."

"Because I don't have anything to wear to school, and Mom has to unpack and iron some of my things because they got all munched in the move. So just you and Dad are going."

"Did I ever mention that you're four foot eleven and a half inches of spoiled rotten kid?"

"I am not. I'm five feet even. Anyway, don't complain. You'll be there with 'little Ginny.' "

"Not me. No one's going to stick me with their daughter. I pick out my own girls. Besides, we've had such a busy week, how come Dad wants to go tonight?"

"You know Dad never misses church," Catherine reminded Jed. "Besides, that's the church where his new boss attends."

"Hey, now what happens if this totally rad guy comes up and wants to meet my cute little sister?" Jed teased.

"Well, you'll just have to show him my picture and tell him to wait in line," Catherine giggled as she opened the door to leave.

"Wait. You forgot to leave me that picture!" Jed called.

"Not this one, you dork. You show this to one living soul and you're history! I'll put scorpions in your shoes, or whatever it is they do out here."

Due to Jed's insistence, he and his dad arrived early to church that evening. They sat two-thirds toward the back of the sanctuary. Jed enjoyed the songs, the sharing, and the teaching—but he spent most of the time searching for the big man and the unseen "little Ginny."

He never did spy any girl that looked like she could belong to such a mom and dad. But he didn't spot the father either. *Maybe they didn't come tonight.* He smiled as he stood to sing the last song. *I guess I'll just have to go home with Dad.*

"There you are, Jed. Glad you came back. I've been telling little Ginny all about you folks."

Where does this guy come from? He just appears out of nowhere at the end of the service.

"I'll be giving Ginny a ride home after the youth group meeting," the big man addressed Jed's father. "Be happy to give the boy a lift home."

Before Jed could beg out, his dad had agreed.

"Listen, Ginny will show Jed where to go. . . . Ginny? Where did she scoot off to? I'll take you over to the Youth Building. Don't worry, we'll have Jed home in about an hour and a half. I guarantee he'll still be in one piece," the big man laughed.

Well, at least that's reassuring.

Jed found himself pushed through the door of a room crammed with seventy to eighty kids. His eyes caught a guy wearing an Ohio State football jersey, so he went over and sat down next to him. He tried to casually peer around. *I will endure the next hour and a half, have an extremely awkward ride home with "little Ginny," and then go to my room and die. Lord, why am I here?*

"Hey, do you like Ohio State football?" Jed finally asked the kid next to him.

"Oh, well, I guess. My dad went to school there so I get a new shirt every Christmas. Are you that new kid from Ohio?"

"Yeah. How did you know?"

"Who else cares about Ohio State? Anyway, my dad's Benjamin Chambers."

"Who?"

"Benjamin Chambers. Doesn't your dad work for SouthWest Steel?'

"Yeah. How did you. . . . "

"My dad is Benjamin Chambers. He owns SouthWest Steel. I'm sure you've heard of him."

"Oh, yeah, sure." Jed let out a phony laugh and turned his attention again to the front of the building. *Actually,* he mumbled to himself, *I never heard of the guy. Lord, how come I lie when I'm so afraid of being embarrassed?*

Up front there were several guys and gals leading songs. His eyes were mostly attracted to a brown-haired girl with a twelve-string guitar. Her radiant smile got his attention. Then he noticed her enthusiasm and her skill with the chords.

Great, Jed thought. *It will be my luck to find a cute girl and she'll be in college, engaged to some 300-pound Sun Devil.*

Right after the songs stopped, the room darkened, and taped music rolled out of some speakers in the back. The front wall revealed three screens for a quick-paced series of slides about the group's camping trip to the Grand Canyon the previous year.

Jed really liked the photography. There were shots of awesome canyon walls, narrow mountain trails, and the majestic Colorado River. He kept thinking about the greatness of the Lord in His creation. He remembered his new 35mm camera. He was definitely ready to sign up to go on the trip.

After the meeting, most of the kids hung around for brownies and something called Desert Rose Punch. Jed kept looking for someone to fit his image of "little Ginny."

Finally he ambled up to the guy in the Ohio State football shirt. "Listen, er . . . remember me? Jed Rivers? What was your name, again?"

"Gary. Gary Chambers."

"Well, Gary, do you happen to know a girl named Ginny?" Jed tried to be cautious. He jammed his hands in the back pockets of his jeans and rocked on the heels of his shoes.

"Ginny? Man, I think we have at least three of them in this group. Hey, Ginny, come here. This dude's new in town and he might be looking for you."

A blonde girl who looked to Jed to be about twelve years old bounced over.

"Hi! I'm Ginny!" She stared at Jed.

"Eh, are you the Ginny I'm supposed to get a ride home with?"

"Yeah!" She smiled, revealing the braces on her teeth.

She sounded too eager to Jed. "I mean, is your dad this really big guy with a grip like the black plague?"

"Oh, no. My dad's in Alaska. But I'm sure my mom could give you a ride—that is, if you live close by . . . like Arizona, Nevada, or New Mexico."

"Relax, Ginny," Gary interrupted. "It sounds like he's looking for Ginny Greenly. She's the only one who has a dad that fits that description. Besides, Jed's much too old for you."

"I'm thirteen and a half!" she retorted with a wiggle of her nose. Jed noticed that she seemed to be always standing on her toes.

"Have you seen Ginny Greenly?" Gary continued.

"Oh, she and some others had to meet with Pastor Dave for a last-minute meeting in his office . . . something about the Grand Canyon trip." Her blonde hair bounced in unison with her chewing gum smack.

Jed cleared his throat. "This Ginny Greenly, is she one of the organizers of that trip?"

"Oh yeah. Her family usually does all the cooking."

"That figures . . ." Jed mumbled.

"Huh?"

"Nothing."

Ginny still stared at Jed. "You have really blue eyes. Are you going on the Spring Break trip?"

"Oh, well . . . I mean, yeah. Thank you. I mean, for the thing about the eyes. Er, no . . . no, I don't think I'll be going on the trip. I mean, it's beautiful. Those slides were great! But it's just that . . . yeah—I'm going to be trying out for the baseball team, and I'm sure I'll be practicing."

"Oh, wow! Are you a baseball player?" Ginny inched closer to Jed, her face only about a foot away from his.

Gary stepped between Jed and Ginny. "Hey, baseball player! Are you going to North West High?"

"Yeah. I got to talk to Coach Stevens in December when we came here to look for a house. He said he was always looking for a left-handed pitcher."

"Hey, I'm a right-handed pitcher at North West. We could use some help. Alright!"

"Wow!" Ginny interrupted again. "I'm left-handed too. Is this awesome, or what? It must be destiny!"

"Ginny, go soak your head in the Desert Rose Punch. You're embarrassing, even if you are my cousin." Gary shoved her toward the refreshments.

13

"See you later, Jed." She raised her eyebrows, which made the freckles on her nose wave. Both boys laughed.

"Hey, don't worry about ball practice. They can't have baseball practice around here during Spring Break, so you can go on that trip. You won't want to miss it. Those slides don't show you half the story. Listen, I've got an extra spot in our four-man tent. You can camp with us."

"Well, thanks. I appreciate it, but I'm not sure if I can get away. With just getting moved in and all, I've got some extra chores around the house. Besides, I need to find a part-time job, you know, to save up some bucks. I'm hoping to buy a car this summer."

"Listen, Jed . . . take it from me . . . you won't want to miss this trip." Gary winked. "Hey, there's Pastor Dave. You can ask him where Ginny Greenly is."

Jed walked over to the short man with a mustache who wore a bright green pullover shirt.

"Eh, excuse me. I'm Jed Rivers, and kind of new here. Have you seen Ginny Greenly? I'm supposed to get a ride home with her."

"Oh, yeah, Jed. Great to meet you. Ginny said she was going outside to find you. Sorry you didn't bump into her. If you don't find her, come on back in. I'll get you another ride."

"Sure. Well, thanks." As Jed walked away he wondered what it would be like to "bump" into little Ginny Greenly.

"Hey, are you going to sign up for the Spring Break trip to the Canyon? It's a great trip," Pastor Dave called out.

"That's what I hear. It looks like I'm going to be tied up with some other things. Maybe after I get settled in, you know, like next year—then I'll be ready for a trip like that."

"Well, if you change your mind, we do have some extra spaces."

"Sure, er, thanks." Jed turned to leave.

"Bye, Jed. . . . Are you sure you don't need a ride?" the blonde Ginny beamed as she ran to his side.

"Oh, no. Thanks. I've got one right out front." He hustled out the door and beelined for the church parking lot.

Kids milled in small groups outside. Some drove off and some waited for their parents. He didn't spot anyone who could be "little Ginny" looking for him, so he parked himself on a big rock beside a water fountain.

If I don't find her in fifteen minutes, I'm going to call Dad, he planned.

Jed caught a glimpse of the girl with the great smile who helped lead the songs. Even in the twilight, he thought she just might be the cutest girl he had ever seen. Her green eyes danced as she talked. And Jed liked the way she dressed. *Not fancy . . . but neat. That's it!* She carried a guitar case over her shoulder, and Jed resisted a momentary impulse to jump up and offer her some help.

After all, if I have to sit here and wait, I might as well visit with someone, he reasoned. *Yeah, but what would I say? Something totally embarrassing like, "My, you certainly play the guitar well."*

After a few more minutes of hesitation, he started toward the girl with the guitar case; but then he spied the young, blonde Ginny coming out of the Youth Building. He spun around and headed for the shadows of some thick landscaping.

"I don't want her to think I need a ride." He scooted along the sidewalk as he mumbled to himself.

When Jed eased out front again, the girl with the guitar case was visiting with someone. As he walked closer he recognized Mr. Greenly.

"There you are, Jed!" the familiar voice blasted across the parking lot.

"Hi. Say, I'm afraid I never found your daughter. I guess there were just too many kids," Jed tried to explain.

"That's what she said. Sorry about that. Well, you kids can visit on the way home. You ready to go Ginny?" he said to the girl with the guitar case.

"You're 'little Ginny'?" Jed blurted out.

"Yeah. Hi! Actually, only my dad calls me 'little Ginny.' Are you Jed?"

He stood motionless for a moment, then blurted, "Are you 15?"

"Oh, yeah. You're Jed, right?"

At that exact moment every thought that Jed Rivers ever housed in his mind vanished. Frantically, he grabbed for something to say. He shifted his weight from one foot to the other.

"Uh . . . you certainly play the guitar well."

"Thanks, Jed." She headed for the car. "It is Jed, isn't it?"

All the way home Jed listened to Mr. Greenly describe the delights of living in Phoenix, while he stared at the back of Ginny's long, curly, brown hair and tried to think of something cool to say.

"Here we are at 1400 Calle Real."

Jed's mind snapped back to attention. "Oh. Hey, thanks, Mr. Greenly."

"Nice to meet you, Jed. We didn't get much of a chance to visit with Daddy doing all the talking. Maybe you can come over sometime," Ginny offered.

"Really? I mean . . . sure!" Jed mumbled.

"Say, Jed, you're going on the youth group trip to the Grand Canyon aren't you?" Mr. Greenly asked.

Jed did a turnabout on the brick sidewalk and leaned back down toward the car. "Oh, yeah. Sounds great. Er . . . you're going aren't you?" he nodded to Ginny.

"Oh, sure," She laughed. "They couldn't get along without me."

Jed nodded in agreement as the Greenlys drove away.

In the house he found the whole family in the living room, sorting through boxes.

"Well, big brother, how did it go?" Catherine asked. "Shall we pack it all back up and head home?"

"Well, Arizona is not Ohio," Jed said with some mystery . . . "but it does have some interesting possibilities . . . some very interesting possibilities."

17

The Great Divide

"Now this is a great way to start the morning!" Mr. Rivers tossed the newspaper on the counter.

"Mom, you didn't sew the button on my royal blue blouse!" Catherine trumpeted above the other voices.

Mrs. Rivers carried a plate of fried eggs over to the table. "What is it, dear?"

"I said, 'I'll just die if I don't get the part of Lady Anne in the play, and I've just got to have. . . .' "

"No, no, Catherine. I was talking to your father," Mrs. Rivers corrected.

Mr. Rivers shoved the paper toward her as he picked up his coffee cup.

"Mother, really! The paper can wait," Catherine whined, trying to comb the tangles out of her wet hair as she squinted at her reflection in the side of the toaster.

"Wow, this is serious, isn't it?" Mrs. Rivers nodded.

"Of course," Catherine sighed. "That's what I've been saying! I really need you to. . . ."

"The Magenta Corporation is closing down the mine at Silver Point? Just how bad is it?"

"Mother! Sometimes I feel like no one is listening to me," Catherine complained.

"No one is listening to you!" Jed sliced into the conversation. "Hand me the peanut butter, please."

"Well. . . ." Mr. Rivers said, picking up the newspaper once more. "The Silver Point mining operation accounted for at least one-fifth of my sales. It's like a twenty percent pay cut, until I can build it back up."

"Mother, Mrs. Clevenger does the casting and her favorite color is blue. I just have to wear blue." Catherine stalked the kitchen waving a half-eaten banana in one hand.

Jed downed his last piece of toast and scooted out of his chair. "Come on, Sis, let's get to school. Besides, I heard Heather Staley say you were a shoo-in for the part." Jed herded his sister out the kitchen door and into the living room.

"She really said I was a shoo-in?" Catherine questioned.

"Yeah. She said you had just the right dignity and charm for the part," Jed chided.

"Really? Wow! Hey, wait . . . Lady Anne is a selfish, wicked, old lady," Catherine reminded him.

"All I know is that someone said you were just right for Lady Anne." Jed was laughing.

Catherine spun towards Jed, rocketing the words: "Well, when I'm a famous actress don't come to me begging for a few thousand to start your carpet cleaning business!"

"Well, famous actress, you might want to take care of that banana stuck on your teeth before you head to school. No telling how many talent scouts might be lurking in the halls of junior high today."

"Man, I guess I'll have to sew the blue button on myself." Catherine scurried across the tile entryway and down the long hall to her bedroom.

Jed started back to the kitchen to tell his folks good-bye, but the tone of the conversation made him retreat.

Maybe this job in the sunbelt isn't all it was supposed to be. He took one last look at his dark brown hair in the tiny mirror next to the front door.

He turned right on Greenway Road, taking long steps, trying to stretch out his tight leg muscles. *Man, I shouldn't have pushed myself so hard in the workout last night. Every muscle is sore.* He punched the button on the light pole and waited for the signal to change at 43rd Avenue.

"Are you ready to go?"

Jed swung around. Ginny Greenly walked up carrying her backpack over her shoulder.

"Oh, well, it's still red—and there's a lot of traffic."

"No, not the signal. I mean, are you all packed for the trip to the Grand Canyon tomorrow?" she said, smiling one of her smiles.

Jed stared for a moment at what he considered to be the greatest smile in North America. "Oh, I will be by tonight. How about you?" Jed tried to stand a little straighter. He felt very physically self-conscious standing next to Ginny. *I knew I should have had a heavier workout last night*, he sighed to himself.

"Yeah, I packed a couple days ago. Then, this morning I decided to redo everything. My room's a mess. I guess guys aren't so flakey, huh?"

"Right. We're quick, decisive, and loyal," Jed blurted out.

"Sounds like Cornpone," she giggled, grabbing Jed's sleeve and pulling him into the now green-lighted crosswalk.

"Cornpone?"

21

"My Cocker Spaniel. He's quick, decisive, and loyal. Are you going to camp with Gary Chambers and those guys?"

"Well, I haven't decided for sure," Jed shrugged.

"Yeah, you're really decisive." Ginny continued, "Well, I think you could be a good influence on that gang."

"What do you mean?"

Ginny sighed. "Oh, it seems like whenever it comes to doing something, well, you know . . . spiritual . . . Gary always cuts out."

Jed's voice grew quiet. "So how come you think I'm going to be a good influence on them?"

"I've heard you pray. I like the way you're open and honest in your prayers. I can tell a lot about a guy by the way he prays . . . if he prays at all."

They finished the hike to North West High discussing nothing more serious than the upcoming Biology test.

"Well, I've got to get to my French class. See you on the bus in the morning."

"Oh, Ginny, say . . . would you like for me to save you a seat on the bus?" Jed tried to force the sentence out of his mind and into an audible response. It just wouldn't come out.

The unsaid line nagged him all day until he finally repeated it out loud, late that night, in his darkened room. *What is there about girls like Ginny that make me feel like an inadequate jerk?*

Jed pushed his sunglasses back over his wavy hair as he stepped into the bus. He waited in the aisle behind a tall, blonde girl named Daffodil.

He noticed an empty seat next to Ginny Greenly, but the girl ahead of him plopped down in it and belted out, "Hey, Ginny, can I sit here?"

"Sure, Daffy." Ginny smiled, then looked up at Jed and shrugged.

"Hey Rivers! Back row for the jocks!"

Jed turned to see Gary Chambers waving his arm from the back of the bus.

"Welcome to the River Rats!" Gary got up so that Jed could slide in toward the window.

"River Rats?" Jed couldn't help repeating.

"That's us," Gary rambled on. "Anyway, you know Mark—and then there's T.J. Bell. T.J. goes to a very private . . . that means expensive . . . school in New Mexico."

"T.J.?" Jed stared at the long-legged guy at the far side of the bus. He had the commanding presence of one who attended a military academy. *Now, that's the way I was trying to look yesterday at the traffic light with Ginny.*

"Hey, one of my best friends in Ohio was named T.J.," Jed offered. "It stood for Thomas Jefferson."

"Nice guess, Rivers," Gary interrupted, "but absolutely nobody knows what the T. J. stands for."

Jed spent most of the four and a half-hour ride staring at the desert and mountains of northern Arizona. Everything looked big, open, rugged, and primitive.

"Hey, Rivers, you want in this game?" Gary broke his concentration. "We're surveying the chicks, you know, rating them from 1 to 10."

"Well, I don't know them very well."

"How about Ginny?" Gary prodded.

"Definitely a 10," Jed nodded.

Mark jumped into the conversation. "I disagree! Ginny's dad guards her like she was solid gold. I wouldn't give her more than a five."

"O.K., Ginny gets a 7.5." Gary continued his cataloging. "Now how about Daffy?"

Jed shook his head, pulled his dark glasses down over his eyes and sank down in the seat, staring out the window. *If Ginny Greenly is a 7.5, the whole world's out of focus.*

When he stepped out of the bus at the rim of the Grand Canyon he was hit by a blast of cold air that swept through the trees.

"What happened to that desert heat?" Jed complained.

"The heat's down there." Gary pointed to the silver thread winding it's way far below the sharp cliffs of the canyon.

"We're going down there?" Jed gasped.

"That's the Colorado River." T.J. added, "I take it this is your first trip to the Canyon?"

"Yeah. Do you come up here often, T.J.?" Jed asked, noticing that T.J. towered over most of the guys, including himself.

"Well, three or four times a year, I suppose. I can't get enough of this place." T.J. ran his fingers through his jet black hair, and took a big gulp of high mountain air. "Come on, we've got to help unload."

Within an hour the bus and truck had been unloaded, and gear was strung all along the top ridge of a canyon trail.

Jed took his sack lunch and sat down next to Ginny and Daffy who were perched in the middle of a big, flat, granite rock.

"Well, how's the newest River Rat?" Ginny teased.

"Man, this is one great view," he said.

"Oh, I bet you say that about all the gorgeous girls," Daffy blurted out.

"No, I mean, the Canyon," Jed blushed, "and the girls."

Turning to Daffy, Jed added, "Man, your hair is the yellowest I've ever seen."

"Yeah, it helps me attract the B's."

"B's?"

"Sure—bums, beachboys and bozos," Daffy kidded. "Now, take Ginny, here. You've got to have a 4.0 and be captain of the football team to even call her on the phone. Right, Gin?"

Ginny looked at Daffy without showing any emotion, "and drive a convertible, don't forget that!"

Suddenly both girls broke into hysterics.

"Hey, Rivers, you old cowboy, come on and pick out your mount!" Gary yelled from the trail.

Jed started for the string of donkeys as Ginny called out, "Don't ride Slow!"

"Don't ride slow?" Jed thought, *"I'll be lucky to ride any way at all."*

Gary, Mark, and T.J. were tying on their gear when Jed got to the trail.

"River Rats, lead the way down the trail," Gary commanded.

"Which one's mine?" Jed looked at several animals who seemed oblivious to the existence of humans.

"That one with the cropped left ear looks about your speed. What do you think, Mark?" Gary looked for agreement.

Mark nodded. "Its name says it all."

"What's its name?"

"Slow. How's that for a peaceful, gentle name?" Gary's voice raced along.

Jed shrugged and grabbed up his gear. *"My first trip down the trail and I get to ride Slow. Huh? Don't ride slow? Slow?"*

"Hey, Gary, er, I don't really like the look of this guy. Think I'll ride this other one instead. What's his name?"

"Headlong," Mark added.

"How did he get his name?"

"You don't want to know," T.J. chimed in and then walked over to where Jed was standing. "Between you and me, Slow is an outlaw. He'll buck off a new rider in less than a minute."

"Hey, you turkeys. You were trying to set me up," Jed protested.

"Nah. Slow is a good donkey. He's usually the first one down to the river, right T.J.?"

"Yeah, and his rider gets there about two hours later." They all laughed as they mounted.

It seemed to Jed an incredibly long time before they reached the bottom of the canyon. His backside ached, his legs were cramped, and sweat was creasing the dust on his face as he reached the end of the trail.

"Isn't it awesome?" T.J. shaded his eyes with his hand and waved the other hand at the steep canyon walls.

"Did you see how narrow that trail was? One false move and Jed Rivers is history," Jed replied.

"That's the beauty of it. Just you and nature. No rules and regulations. No man-made barriers. I love it down here." Suddenly, T.J. turned and ran across the sand to the water's edge, screaming at the top of his lungs, his voice echoing and reechoing.

Jed helped Gary, Mark, and T.J. set up camp. Their tent was pitched away from the campground up against a shallow cave in the towering cliff. The campsite was buzzing with confusion as tents and kids sprawled everywhere. Finally he found Ginny, who was sitting near the water, strumming her guitar. She had changed into a red tank-top and had a red and white bandana tied around her neck. Jed felt sloppy in his faded, dirty, Chicago Cubs T-shirt.

She spoke first. "Sometimes everything in the world gets so . . . you know, confusing. I love coming down here. I think this must be where the Lord comes when He gets disgusted with us and wants a change of scenery."

"Are you going to sing tonight?" Jed asked.

"Oh, I'll just lead some choruses I guess. What do the River Rats have planned? They usually do something funny, or embarrassing, or crude . . . or all three." Ginny smiled.

"Nah . . . we're not planning anything," Jed assured her.

"See, you've already had a good influence on them." Ginny jumped up and walked back with him to camp.

Jed wandered back up to the white tent with the red letters "R. R." splattered across the side.

"Gather 'round, River Rats, and listen to the opening night kick-off," Gary called out. "We slip out during the study and go back to our tent and get into costume."

"I'm not going to dress up like a giant marshmallow again," Mark complained.

"No, no. It's different. Look what I brought! Wigs! Brown ones, black ones, and especially bright blonde ones!"

"What are they for?" Mark mockingly tried on a blonde one.

"Exactly . . . exactly. This year we impersonate the girls. Whose blonde hair does that look like?"

"Daffy's!" T.J. laughed.

"Correcto! See, we all sneak back here during the study, and then, soon as it's over, we run up to the front and squeal 'Pastor Davy, will you roast my marshmallow?' You know, stuff like that. What do you think?"

"It's crude," Mark laughed. "I love it. We'll do it."

"Great! Let's go eat."

"Is he serious?" Jed whispered to T.J.

"At least we're not mermaids. I almost froze that year." T.J. shook his head and started across the sand. Jed ducked back into the tent pulling on his newest shirt, then sprinted to catch up with the others. He spent most of supper time listening to all of Gary's plans for the evening's excitement.

It was pitch dark by the time the Bible study started, and there was no moonlight shining down in the canyon. Jed saw Mark peel off of the group. In a couple minutes Gary did the same. He waited a little while and then followed them into the darkness.

Halfway back to the tent he stopped and sighed. *I am not going to do this.*

He was still standing there when T.J. bumped into him.

"Jed? Hey, what's up?"

Jed looked back to the campfire. "I think I'll just pass on the night's activity. I'll let you guys have all the fun."

T.J. grabbed Jed's shoulder. "Just some friendly advice. Gary Chambers can get real vindictive."

"This isn't that big a deal . . . is it?"

"It is to Gary," T.J. cautioned. "Believe me, it's not worth the hassle he'll cause."

"I'll have to take the chance. Think I'll go down near the river." Jed made his way toward the sound of the water.

A moment of silence was broken with T.J.'s whisper, "Wait up! I'm coming with you."

"What? And face the revenge of the chief River Rat?"

"Oh, Gary will probably leave me alone."

"Yeah, how come?"

"Well, for one thing, I'm on the boxing team at the military school. I could bash his face in."

"And the other thing?" Jed questioned.

"My dad's richer than his dad. Money seems to impress Gary."

"Your dad's richer than Benjamin Chambers and SouthWest Steel?"

"Yeah, by a longshot. But you don't want to hear that story."

Jed scooted down in the sand by the river's edge and leaned against a rock. T.J. perched against the same rock from the other side. Jed looked up at the brilliant star-painted sky that hung wedged atop the black walls of the canyon.

Finally he interrupted the silence. "Hey, I want to hear the true story of T.J. Bell. How rich is your dad?"

"Did you read in the newspapers this summer about the natural gas strike down in south Texas?"

"Yeah . . . 'Belt City is Booming.' Is your dad in on that?" Jed questioned.

"Well, it's not Belt City, it's Bell City. And that's my dad's town."

"You mean they named the town after your dad?"

"I mean, my dad named the town after himself. He owns it—town, gas wells, cattle ranches, the whole smear. My mom was from Texas. We lived there until I was five, then my mom died. So Dad moved us back to where he grew up."

"Hey, I'm sorry about your mom." Jed searched for something to say. "How did it happen?"

"A plane crash. Mom and Dad were flying down to Mexico. The plane went down in the desert. Dad made it. Mom didn't. That's all there is."

"Do you think about it much anymore?"

"Yeah. Every now and then I really miss her . . . but . . . hey, I can hardly remember what she was like. After all, I was only five."

Jed tried to imagine what it would be like if it had been his own mother who died. Deep in empathetic thought, he was silent.

T.J. continued, "Anyway, Dad's a great guy. He really tries to do things for me. Only trouble is, my whole life is planned for me. He chooses the schools, the vacations, the careers. That's why I love it down here—because it's just me and the elements. Kind of raw, rugged and unplanned. Know what I mean?"

Jed stretched his arms. "Yeah, it's great. You just look up at that sky and you've got to think about how great God must be. Planets, stars, moons, canyons, rivers . . . He can handle all of it. Man, that's power."

"Well . . . not quite powerful enough," T.J. mumbled.

Jed sat up and turned toward T.J., who was out of sight behind the darkness of the boulder. "What do you mean?"

"I mean, she was one neat Christian lady. You ought to read her diary. Anyway, it's not fair."

Jed searched for something to say. He felt like he should defend God, but no wise words came to mind. Finally he just blustered, "You sound mad at God."

"Oh, I used to be mad. Now, I just, well, figure we aren't suppose to be able to know much about Him. I kind of just gave up trying after a few years of struggle. Have you got God figured out, Jed?"

"There are some things about Him I'm sure of," Jed added.

"What's Jed short for?"

"Huh?"

"I'm changing the subject. Isn't Jed a nickname?"

Jed relaxed against the rock. "You going to tell me what T.J. stands for?"

"Nah. You'd just laugh."

"No, really—what is it?"

"You've got to promise not to tell anyone. It's kind of a secret thing, you know?"

"OK," Jed assured. "I won't laugh and I won't tell anyone."

"Texas Jack. My real name is Texas Jack Bell. Now what about the Jed?"

"You're teasing me, right? You're not serious?"

"You're laughing—I'm serious—and what about the Jed?"

"Texas Jack? Nobody names their kid Texas Jack!"

"Look, it was my mom's dad's name. Tell me about Jed."

"It's short for Jedediah. Jedediah Wilson Rivers."

"Well, it's a standoff. I think we both got hooked," T.J. laughed. "Look, you know all about me—so, now tell me about the Rivers family."

While they stared up at the stars, Jed rambled about life in Ohio, and how they ended up in Phoenix.

"So does your dad like working for Ben Chambers at SouthWest Steel?" T.J. shot his question out into the night.

"I guess it's not all he thought it would be. Something about Silver Point closing down."

"Silver Point? That's one of the biggest copper mines in the world," T.J. whistled.

"Yeah. Well, I think my dad's kind of discouraged."

"Is he ready to move back to Ohio?"

"No way. I mean, I don't think so. Anyway, moms and dads always come through, right?"

"That's what people tell me." T.J. stood up and threw a stone in the water.

"You think it's time we headed back?" Jed asked.

"I suppose. Don't forget I warned you about the wrath of the chief River Rat."

They worked their way along the river and then through the main part of camp where most of the youth group were still roasting marshmallows. Jed stopped by the campfire, next to Ginny.

"Hey, I knew you could do it," she grinned.

"What?"

"Keep the River Rats out of trouble. What did you do? Chain them down?" she laughed.

"They didn't wear the wigs? I mean, I didn't have anything to do with it, did I?" Jed addressed the question to T.J. who was standing next to him.

"We'll see soon enough." T.J. rubbed his hands over the fire and turned to leave.

Jed and T.J. hiked back up to their tent and cave. A small light from a dying campfire flickered against the wall of the canyon.

"Oh, this is cute, Jed! The tent's gone!"

"It's what?"

"The tent, all our gear, and Gary and Mark are gone!" T.J. kicked in the sand.

The canyon breeze felt colder and the night looked blacker as Jed jammed his hands in his pockets and flopped down in the shallow cave, leaning against the back of the hard rock cliff.

"Well," T.J. shrugged, "welcome to Arizona."

Jed shook his head and moaned, "River Rats. The name says it all."

Crashing In

"You know what really burns me?" Mr. Rivers continued—"Chambers even called me into his office and wanted to know why you were picking on his kid."

"That's crazy!" Jed exploded. "Gary and Mark got mad because T.J. and I wouldn't play it their way. So they took off down the river with all our gear."

"Did you ride out in a helicopter?" Catherine asked.

"No, no, I told you . . . Gary and Mark tried to climb up the side of the canyon in the dark, and Mark fell and sprained his ankle. Only Mark and Gary were flown out."

"Chambers was way out of line . . . way out of line," Jed's dad mumbled as he stormed toward the kitchen.

"Is Gary Chambers really a jerk?" Catherine whispered.

"Yeah, well, I . . . " Jed caught himself. Nothing positive came to mind. "That's one way to describe him."

"You'll be pleased to know," Catherine announced, "that while you were out ruining the Canyon trip, I was selected to be Lady Anne in the school play."

Jed laughed. "What happened, didn't anyone else try out?"

"It so happens that Barry Wright tried out."

"A guy? A guy tried out for Lady Anne?"

"He has this high, weird voice and he couldn't get any of the boys' parts."

"So, other than that, what's happened in the week that I was gone?"

"Well, this guy in English slipped me a note about. . . ."

"No, I mean around here. At home. You know, important stuff."

"Oh, Mom and Dad keep having long conversations about his job. Dad's really depressed about it. Anyway, you picking on the boss's son didn't help," Catherine added.

"Look, I didn't . . . " Jed sighed in frustration. Then he did what he always did when things seemed to be spinning out of control—he went out into the garage and lifted weights.

Jed spent most of Monday trying to avoid Gary Chambers while searching for Ginny Greenly. At lunch he spotted her. She was wearing a green blouse that made her eyes sparkle. Jed thought it incredible that she was sitting alone on a bench next to the baseball field. He walked straight up to her.

"Hi, Jed. I hear you start baseball practice today," Ginny said as she shielded her eyes from the sun.

"Yeah. It will be good to get started and meet some new guys. I'm not doing too well so far. I think I flunked River Rat School!"

"Well, it's your gain. You didn't fit in with that gang," Ginny added.

"Hey, T.J. is solid. In fact, I wish he went to North West."

"Yeah. So do half the girls here. Tall, dark, handsome . . . and rich!"

"You mean lonesome, trapped and shy," Jed blurted out. "Anyway, are you one of those girls who have wished T.J. was at North West?"

"Maybe," she grinned. "I am glad that Jed Rivers is here."

"Oh yeah? How come?"

"Because we need a left-handed pitcher on the baseball team and I hear you're really good."

"Who did you hear that from?"

"Ginny Rinaldi. She's that blonde junior high girl at church. Do you know her? Hey, there's the bell. Call me and tell me how practice went."

"Really?"

"Yeah, really," she smiled.

Sometime during the past hour the sun had gone down and Jed's room darkened as he lay on his bed, listening to the stereo. Baseball practice had not gone well. Coach Stevens had allowed Jed to pitch to only three batters. The assistant coach had told Jed just to take it easy, toss some strikes and let them get some hits. The next thing he knew, he was out catching fly balls with the junior varsity outfielders.

Man, they didn't give me a chance. It's like they made up their mind before I could show them what I had! Welcome to Arizona, Rivers. Gary Chambers is behind this. I don't know what happened, but somehow he's. . . .

"Hey! What's going on!" he said out loud. Jed covered his eyes as his bedroom door swung open and the bright overhead light pierced the room.

"And this is Jed's room," Catherine announced, "and this is my brother, Jed. I think you know him, right Ginny?"

Ginny? Jed swung off the bed and strained to adjust to the light.

"Oh yeah. We're friends. Hi, Jed!"

He recognized the voice immediately. "Ginny Rinaldi? What's she doing here?"

"Ginny volunteered to help me learn my lines," Catherine smiled. "She just wanted a tour of the house, that's all."

"Well, this is the dungeon, so turn out the light, huh?"

"Mr. Personality tonight. Did your girlfriend dump you?"

"Does Jed have a girlfriend?" Ginny asked Catherine.

"No, I don't. Anyway, forget it. Is Dad home yet?"

"He's not coming home. He had to make an emergency trip to El Paso, Texas. Mom said they decided to switch everything around at work. Anyway, she's in the kitchen all bummed-out, and you're pouting in your bedroom. I think I'm the only normal one in the family. Come on, Ginny. Lady Anne beckons us to tea."

It was five days later before Jed got to talk to his dad, and two weeks later before he got up the nerve to talk to Coach Stevens. After watching most of the practice from the sidelines, Jed shoved his hat to the back of his head, and intercepted the coach as he headed to the gym.

"Coach, when we talked back in December you sounded like you needed a left-hander."

"Rivers, when I talked to you last winter I didn't know you were going to come in here and alienate half the team. We don't need some eastern hot shot who's not a team player."

"Alienate the team? I don't even know the team!"

"Well, they know you. Chambers, Whitney, Jessup, and others have told me about your griping and criticizing. I don't build teams that can't get along with each other."

"They said what?" Jed pulled off his hat and waved it as he continued. "And you believed them?" he shouted.

Coach Stevens' face flushed with anger. "Well, if you're going to play on my team you'll have to start by putting in ten laps. . . . Yell at me again and the only team you'll make at North West is the chess team."

"Look, Dad, I'm dropping out of baseball, that's all. I've just had it with Arizona vengeance," Jed repeated his position.

"Do you know what it looks like?" His dad pushed away from the supper table and folded his arms. "It looks like some kid from the East, who spent his life being the favorite son of River Heights baseball, has met some stiff competition and now wants to throw in the towel."

"Yeah, well that's not true. Gary Chambers is just trying to get back at me, and I really don't need the hassle. I thought you'd see that."

"I do see it, Jed. I only said what it looks like to others," Mr. Rivers explained. "Remember what we talked about right before that Little League Championship game a few years ago? You were so nervous you were sick to your stomach. I distinctly remember your prayer about letting the Lord have His way with your baseball ability."

"Sure, but I was just a kid. I mean, this thing with Gary is just out of proportion. Sometimes I wish we were back in Ohio, know what I mean?"

"Ohio?" Catherine flew into the conversation. "I get a big theatrical break, and you talk of Ohio!"

"Dad, can I go over to Ginny Greenly's?" Jed asked.

Catherine threw up her hands, "You can't. . . . I promised Ginny Rinaldi that you'd be home."

"You what?"

"Look, she has this thing about you. I mean, it's really kind of stupid, but she's one of those girls who's boy crazy, you know?"

Catherine was still talking to him when Jed left and began walking over to Ginny's house.

At least Ginny will understand. She warned me about those guys. That lucky T.J.'s in New Mexico. He doesn't have to put up with this junk.

"Hi, Mr. Greenly. Is Ginny home?"

It was the first time Jed saw Mr. Greenly without a smile. He looked twice as massive. "Rivers, I think you've got a lot of growing up to do, and I suggest you do it with someone besides my daughter!"

The front door slammed and Jed found himself looking around the yard. Jed sat on the curb in front of Ginny's house for awhile. He just picked up little pebbles along the sidewalk and tossed them toward the center of the street. His thoughts and emotions raced from one extreme to another. Finally, he got up, glanced back at the Greenly's front door, then started the long, slow walk home. He felt like yelling.

Jed watched the hot desert sun slip into the horizon as he walked past the landscaped saguaro cactus that guarded his driveway. *This is where the cowboy rides into the sunset.*

Catherine met him at the door.

"Well, thanks to you, Ginny Rinaldi went home without hardly helping me. She seemed really miffed that you weren't here. Sometimes I think she has it made being an only child. I mean, I don't know why you couldn't have just. . . ."

"Catherine!" The tone of Jed's voice silenced his sister. It was pitch dark when he entered his room, and he didn't bother turning on a light until morning.

"Jed, are you mad at me?" Catherine cautiously stuck her head in his room.

Jed rustled through his closet to find a blue and green print shirt. "Hey, look Cath, I'm sorry. Everything's crashing in on me. Just don't crowd me. OK? I've got some things to figure out, and I'd rather not have junior high Ginny hanging out at my door. OK?"

"Sure, Jed. She can be kind of pushy, can't she?"

"If you promise not to line me up with girlfriends, I'll promise not to line you up with boyfriends. What do you say?"

"You've got it. Hey, are things really that bad?"

"Yeah. Are you still ready to move back to Ohio?"

"No way. That was weeks ago. You're not wanting to give up on Arizona are you?"

"The thought has become increasingly more popular," Jed sighed.

"Hey, it will get better. Listen, I didn't really mean what I said."

"About what?"

"About not wanting you to line up any boyfriends for me. I mean, if someone like T. J. Bell wanted to meet me, I wouldn't mind if you sort of . . . you know . . . fixed it up."

"T.J.? All the girls like T.J. If he weren't in New Mexico I'd invite him over tonight."

"Really? To talk with me?"

"No, to talk to me." Jed grabbed the shirt and some jeans and headed to the shower.

He was putting his books into his locker when Ginny Greenly pinned him with a barrage of questions.

"What in the world did you say in those letters? How come my dad's mad at you? Why did you come over and make it worse last night?"

"What letters? What are you talking about? I didn't say anything to your dad last night."

"Well, he absolutely forbids me to see you or talk to you. He mumbled something about you being mentally unbalanced. He said you were a wolf in sheep's clothing. He even hinted that you showed no evidence of really being saved. What did you say in those letters?"

"WHAT LETTERS!" Jed slammed his locker closed and spun around to face Ginny. He could feel the veins in his neck strain with tension. She stepped back and looked frightened. Jed noticed others in the hallway staring at them.

He lowered his voice and sighed. "Ginny, I don't have any idea what's going on. I'm sorry I yelled. Can we talk at lunch? I don't even know what to apologize for."

"I can't." She looked down at her feet. "I've got a dentist appointment."

"How about tonight?"

"My dad wouldn't let me."

"Not even on the phone?"

"Especially on the phone."

"Can I meet you at the library?"

"No, it just complicates everything."

"How about tomorrow night? I'm serious. I need to talk."

"Tomorrow I work with the junior high youth group. But if you wanted to come help, maybe we'd have a chance to visit."

"When and where?"

"7:00 p.m. at the Rinaldi's."

"I'll be there."

"See you tomorrow."

"You can count on it." Jed rubbed his hand through his brown hair and took a big deep breath. He walked down the hall, alone, toward his next class.

Jerk. I acted like a jerk.

For the next day and a half, he practiced what he was going to say to Ginny.

"How was baseball today?" his mom questioned.

"Don't ask."

"I hear you're going with Catherine tonight."

"Yeah, they needed some of us to help with Junior High. Besides, I need to talk to Ginny," Jed admitted.

"Is something wrong?"

"Yeah. But it's really weird. I mean, I can't talk to you about it because I don't even know what it is."

"Mother! Mother, listen . . . this is really dumb. My own brother is going to *my* youth group meeting." Catherine scooted into the room. "What are my friends going to say?"

"I know what Ginny Rinaldi will say," Mrs. Rivers smiled.

43

"I mean the guys. What will the guys say? 'Oh, here's Catherine's big brother. He's come to keep her out of trouble.' "

"You won't hear them say anything if you don't get ready in five minutes," Mrs. Rivers reminded.

"Five minutes? My hair is horrible. . . . Mother, help me!" Catherine moaned.

Jed started to his room, but turned to answer the telephone instead. A moment later he called out to his mom.

"Dad said he would be real late, something about a big meeting with the boss. Must be serious—he asked us to pray for him." Jed headed back to his room.

"Catherine, we're leaving right now," Mrs. Rivers announced as she dug in her purse for her keys.

"I'm not going! My hair is awful!" Catherine whined.

"Well, I think it looks just like that blonde nurse on the television show last night." Mrs. Rivers held the back door open.

"No kidding?"

"Do mothers lie? Jed, we're leaving. . . . " The ring of the telephone interrupted her words.

Jed and Catherine were standing by the back door when Mrs. Rivers summoned Jed to the phone.

"It's T.J. Bell. Remember, we have to hurry."

Jed raced to the phone and shouted out a greeting. "T.J.! Hey, where are you?"

"In New Mexico, at school. Listen, Jed, you got a minute?" T.J. sounded worried.

"Uh, sure. I mean, listen. . . ." Jed searched around the room as if looking for an answer. "Hey, I was just going out the door to a youth group meeting. I needed to talk to Ginny. Can I call you back later?"

"How much later?"

"Oh, say, uh . . . about two hours?"

"Nah . . . it's OK. Just a long shot. I sort of knew you would be busy," T.J.'s voice faded.

"Jed! Come on, you turkey!" Catherine's highest soprano complaint shot from the kitchen.

"Wait a minute!" Jed yelled.

"Listen, T.J., what's this about?" Jed felt uneasy asking.

"I need you to fly to New Mexico tonight," T. J.'s voice broke. "Dad took a helicopter to an off-shore oil rig down in the gulf on Monday morning. He never showed up. They can't find any trace of him."

"Jed, we really must go." Mrs. Rivers was insistent.

"Uh, yeah." Jed fought for wisdom. "Mom, go on without me."

"T.J., I've got plenty of time to talk. What's all this about?" Jed slumped to the floor, still holding the phone.

"Catherine," he shouted toward the kitchen, "tell Ginny that T.J. needs to talk and I can't make it. She'll understand."

T.J. continued the conversation. "Listen, Jed, a couple of guys from my dad's company called me this afternoon and said he hasn't been seen for two days. I wanted to go home to Phoenix, but they said I might need to fly down to Texas, so I should just stay put."

"Yeah, but he flies a lot, right?" Jed tried to console. "He'll be OK."

"Jed, I called and got a ticket for you to fly down here on the 8:30 plane. Would your folks let you come? It's Apache Trails, flight number 63. You will get to Las Cruces by 10:10. I'll meet you there."

"T.J., my folks aren't home right now."

"Remember when we were down in the canyon and you said there were some things about God you knew for sure?"

"Yeah."

"Well, today I don't think I know anything for sure."

"T. J., I'll do everything I can to get there. Hang on."

"Man, I really appreciate it."

Jed's packed suitcase was sitting by the back door when his mom walked in twenty minutes later.

"Mom, I've got to get to New Mexico. T.J.'s in trouble. It's an emergency and I've got to get to Sky Harbor and catch an 8:30 flight."

"What? Is this some sort of a game? Is this part of the junior high youth activity?"

"Mom, can I explain it to you in the car on our way to the airport? If you think it's crazy then you can just drive me back home."

Jed rattled out the whole story to his mom as they traveled south through the city. He told of T.J.'s loss of his mom when he was only five, and the loneliness in T.J.'s life.

"Mom, he needs a friend . . . right now, tonight. It sort of looks like I'm supposed to be that friend. I mean, he's got absolutely no one to turn to. Can I go?"

She pulled into the terminal in front of Apache Trails Airline.

"Jed, I just don't feel right about making such a decision without talking to your dad, and he's tied up with Mr. Chambers."

"Mom," Jed paused, "I really, really need to do this."

"I know . . . I know." She took a deep breath and sighed. "OK. Listen . . . you call Dad and me as soon as you get into Las Cruces. Have you got any money?"

"T.J. paid for the ticket, and I've got $20."

"Here, take another $20. Jed, be careful . . . act smart . . . call us."

Jed gave his mom a hug, grabbed his suitcase, and hurried into the terminal.

The plane bounced it's way into the night as it crossed the New Mexico border and headed down for the Rio Grande. The roar of the plane gave Jed time to think. Somehow, his troubles seemed fairly minor when placed alongside T.J.'s.

His tall, military school attending friend met him at the airport.

"T.J., any news?" Jed hurried through the crowded terminal.

"The seas are too rough and they've called off the search. I guess that's news."

"Listen, my suitcase is dark blue with an old Ohio State bumper sticker on the side of it. Can you grab it for me? I need to call home and report in."

Jed fumbled with the phone, finally getting the operator to place a collect call.

"Hi, Catherine. It's me. Can I talk to Mom or Dad?"

"Jed? Are you really in New Mexico?"

"Yeah. Listen, I need to talk to the folks."

"I don't think this is a good time?" Catherine cautioned. "Dad came home and said he quit his job. They are upstairs talking, and I think Mom is crying."

"Quit his job? Oh . . . wow! Listen. Tell them that I got to New Mexico just fine and I'll call them first thing in the morning."

"Right. Eh, Jed?"

"Yeah?"

"I sort of wish you were here tonight, you know?"

"Hey, me too. Mom and Dad will work things out. Listen, did you get that message to Ginny?"

"Sure. She said it was no problem. But I could tell it bothered her."

"You could? How?"

"Something about the freckles on her nose. I mean, it's sort of funny, but they kind of give away how she is feeling."

"Ginny doesn't have any freckles."

"Doesn't have freckles? Are you blind? They're clear across her face."

"Ginny Greenly doesn't have freckles," Jed insisted.

There was a long pause before Catherine came back on the phone.

"Ginny Greenly? Your message about T.J., and that you'd talk to her later, was for Ginny Greenly?"

"Of course it was for Ginny Greenly!" Jed was almost shouting. "Who did you think it was for?"

"Eh . . . Ginny Rinaldi?" Catherine bit her lip. "Jed, I've got to go. Talk to me tomorrow."

"Catherine!'

"Jed, I'm serious. I'm going to throw up. You know I can't handle all this pressure. Good-bye."

He turned to see T.J. walking toward him, carrying his suitcase.

Lord, this would be a really good time to wake up from a horrible dream. Jed took a deep breath and hung up the phone.

"Jed," T.J. looked him right in the eyes, "you're coming here tonight is just about the greatest thing anybody ever did for me. Thanks."

The two remained silent as they walked out into the cool New Mexico night.

Smooth Sailing

The New Mexico Technical Military Academy did not look anything like what Jed had imagined. He had thought it would be an old army post—with barracks, rustic mess halls, and barren parade grounds. He was wrong.

"So this is where T.J. Bell has to rough it during the school year?" Jed kidded as he flopped down in a big, overstuffed, leather chair that was scooted up close to a colossal circular fireplace in the center of the main lounge. "This room is as big as the lodge at East Glacier."

"Have you ever been up there in the winter?" T.J. asked.

"To Glacier National Park? Nah. We went by there a couple summers ago on our way to Seattle. Man, that's some road over the pass," Jed continued.

"It's called "Going to the Sun" highway," T.J. added. "The Indians figured they were closer to the gods up there."

"Hey, it must work." Jed continued, "I mean, I always feel close to God when I'm up in the mountains."

"Or down in the canyons?" T.J. questioned.

"Yeah, there too."

T.J. took an iron rod and stirred the coals in the fire. Without saying anything, he pulled off his black cowboy boots, plopped down on a chair next to Jed, and stretched his long legs out on the hearth.

"Well, I don't feel very close to God right now," T.J. sighed. "He won't let anything happen to my dad, right? I mean, it's just not fair."

"T.J., I don't understand it either. But remember, I didn't say I know everything," Jed added. "Isn't there anything you can do besides waiting? I mean, aren't there some relatives to talk to? You know . . . something?"

"Not really. My grandma's in a nursing home down in Texas, and I've got an uncle somewhere, but we haven't heard from him in years. It's always sort of been me and Dad." T.J. stood up with his back to the fire.

Jed sat and stared at the flames for a long time. *Lord, there is absolutely nothing I can say to T.J. How come I never have answers for the tough questions?*

"It's not fair, Jed. I don't want to go through all of this again." T.J. turned away from Jed and faced the fire, eyes wet with emotion and mirroring confusion. "OK, Rivers, tell me everything you know for sure about God. I think it's time for me to get a refresher course."

It was almost midnight when Jed started talking. He had no idea where the best place to begin was, so he told how he had discovered the reality of God in his own life through a personal commitment to Jesus Christ. Then the subject bounced from right and wrong . . . to good and evil . . . to man's will and God's will . . . to sin and punishment . . . and heaven and hell. It was sometime around 2:30 a.m. when the conversation started slowing down.

Jed noticed that the fire had gone out, and everyone had long since deserted them.

"Don't we need to get some sleep?" Jed stretched and yawned.

"Oh, hey . . . go on up to the room. Sure. I think I'd better stick around down here. You know, there might be a phone call."

"If you're staying here, I'm staying here," Jed insisted.

Both boys stretched out in the big leather chairs that surrounded the fireplace. Their conversation grew increasingly sporadic as they dozed off. It was a third voice that jolted them awake and sent chills down their backs.

"T.J., there's a telephone call for you."

Jed jumped to his feet to see a grey-haired man in a maroon bathrobe make the announcement and then begin to shuffle back to the west end of the huge lounge.

"Come on, Jed. I need you along."

"Are you sure, T.J.? I could just. . . . " Jed changed his mind halfway through the sentence and raced behind his friend.

"Dad? DAD! Where are you? Are you OK? What happened?"

Tears were streaming down T.J.'s face. And he didn't bother to wipe them off.

Jed couldn't hold back his own tears. He turned and walked toward the circular fireplace. *No matter what T.J. says, there are just times when you need to be alone with your dad.*

It was about ten minutes later when T.J. came running back across the lounge and slapped Jed on the back.

"Where is he, T.J.? Is he OK?"

53

"Listen, this is incredible. A storm came up Monday morning and caught him halfway out to the oil platform. He was going to head back but the helicopter started cutting out, like it was low on fuel. Well, he brought it down and landed the thing, in rough seas, right on top of a Panamanian freighter. He found that none of the crew spoke English. When they finally communicated, he learned that they all thought he was coming to rescue them, because they had lost their power and were floating at sea. Anyway, this morning they all washed up at some little island off Mexico."

"So he's OK, and everything?" Jed asked.

"Yeah, no problems, except he was really worried about me." T.J. was starting to relax and smile.

"Where is he now?"

"At some Mexican airport. . . . He's headed to Phoenix, and wants us to meet him there in the morning."

"Us?" Jed raised his eyebrows.

"Yeah. I told him how you flew down to Las Cruces to be with me. He said, 'T.J. hold on to that Jed. A guy only gets a couple of good friends like that in a lifetime.' Anyway, he wants to meet you. His plane will get to Phoenix about 1:30 tomorrow, so we'd better get some sleep before we fly home."

"Did you reach your mom?" T.J. called out before Jed could get over to the stables.

"Yeah. Your problems are over, and mine are getting bigger. Dad got fed up with Ben Chambers and quit his job; my sister Catherine is threatening to run away from home if I come back mad at her; and

Ginny Greenly won't speak to me because she thinks I wrote her some weird letters."

"Other than that, how are things?" T.J. laughed. "Come on, I promised you a tour of the school before we left."

"Are you sure the best way to tour is by horseback?"

"Trust me." T.J. kicked the flanks of his horse and left Jed in the dust. Within a half hour they were high above the academy, staring down at the Rio Grande Valley.

"This is my favorite place." T.J. pointed across the horizon. "See those mountains in the east? Those are the San Andres Mountains. Dad and I discovered gold up there once, about three years ago."

"Gold? You guys have a gold mine?" Jed shook his head.

"No, we just discovered some gold in one of the streams up there when we were on a hunting trip, so Dad bought the property. He says one of these days we should get back up there and see if it's worth developing. Anyway, look out across the valley" T.J. continued. "Can't you just feel the freshness of the air? Every time I get depressed, I just ride up here and sit awhile. I think everyone needs a place like this."

"Yeah. I used to have this patch of woods, back in Ohio. I'd ride my bike out there and sit right in the middle of it, pretending like I was Lewis and Clark, out to discover the Northwest Passage or something."

"Jed, do you miss Ohio?"

"Yeah, sort of. I guess I miss my friends most of all. Did I ever tell you I have a friend in Ohio named T.J.?"

"Thomas Jefferson something-er-other, right?"

"Right. Anyway, since Dad quit his job, we might have to move back to Ohio to find work."

"Well, how about not doing that for a while, because I'm just beginning to enjoy having a friend I can trust," T.J. admitted. "Last one back to the barn has to rub down the horses!"

It was one race Jed didn't even try to win. He learned on the way up that Texas Jack Bell was born and raised on horseback. Jed doubted if there were more than five kids in New Mexico who could outride T.J.

The flight back to Phoenix was completely different than the one Jed had taken the night before. This time the ride was smooth, the view spectacular, and the conversation upbeat. The normally quiet T.J. never stopped talking.

"You know, Jed, I was listening to what you were saying about God last night. It really made a difference. I mean, before I talked to you, I sort of made this deal with God. I told Him if He would let my dad be alive, then I'd know He was real. But something about what you were saying made me change my mind. About the time we dozed off to sleep, I revised the deal. I said, 'Lord, if You can keep my faith strong, right through the middle of all this, then I'll know You are real.' Anyway, it probably doesn't make a lot of sense, but it sure did help me."

"Yeah, I understand. Everything doesn't always go right, even when you're really trying to do things right," Jed added. "T.J., do you know Ginny Greenly very well?"

"Not really. I mean, I'm away at school most of the year. Besides, I don't visit much with girls. Why?"

"Well, she and her dad have this idea that I've been sending her some gross letters or something. I can't even get close enough to find out the problem. Man, they sure were quick to expect the worst from me."

"Oh, don't take it personally. Ginny's dad is known for being extremely protective, especially of his 'little Ginny,' " T.J. counseled.

"Anyway," Jed continued, "I thought maybe you could find out what's going on with Ginny and her dad."

"I'll give it a shot, but I'm warning you—I'm not very good at diplomacy," T.J. grinned.

As the boys grabbed their gear and made their exit off the plane, Jed felt overwhelmed by all of his hassles still unsolved. He was off in a daze, thinking about Ginny, when T.J. grabbed his arm and pulled him across the terminal.

"Jed . . . hey, there's my dad!" T.J. called.

Jed looked up to see a tall man with an old, beat-up, black, beaver felt cowboy hat pushed to the back of his head. Jed stepped back and watched his friend and father embrace and exchange greetings. Then an arm on his shoulder spun him around.

"Hey, remember us?" Jed's dad gave him a hug.

"Dad! Mom! Oh, yeah. It's just that T.J. was so worried, I almost forgot."

There was a steady line of introductions and continuous conversation between T.J., his father, Jed and his parents, all the way to the baggage claim area and into the parking lot.

"T.J., I've got to get to baseball practice, call me tonight if you get a chance."

"You've got it. Listen, dude, I owe you one. Anytime, anyplace—you give me a call and I'll be there. I mean it."

"Yeah, well I just might wait until the night of the Military Banquet or something," Jed kidded.

"I'll be there."

"I know. . . . I'll talk to you later."

Jed felt ten years older than he had only the day before at baseball practice. In the span of twenty-four hours he had been on a physical and emotional roller coaster, and he was just plain worn out. For once it didn't bother him at all that he was relegated to the bench for the afternoon scrimmage.

The first and second squads were playing each other, and Jed wasn't at all sure which team he would end up on.

"Rivers! Loosen up. I want you to pitch next inning." The coach's voice bounced down the steps and into the dugout. Jed hurried to comply. Not until he had thrown a dozen pitches did he learn that he would be on the second squad. Normally, he would have been hyped-up at the chance to prove himself. Today he was just too tired to care.

As the second team took the field, Jed went to the mound. He didn't think to scout out who the first batter would be, but a familiar voice broke the concentration.

"Well, hot-shot, give me your best throw!"

Oh, great. I'm worn out and Gary Chambers is the batter!

Jed decided to throw Gary some junk. After a couple of curves, and an off-speed slider, the count was two balls and one strike. One voice inside Jed told him to throw the big roundhouse curve, and another voice warned him against it. If it worked, Gary would look silly . . . if it didn't, Gary would probably get beaned and charge the mound. Jed decided to listen to the first voice.

The pitch started out for Gary's head and he threw himself flat on the ground. But the big curve took hold and broke down to the plate. The assistant coach, who was acting as umpire, called it a strike. Gary was deep red as he dusted himself off and glared at Jed.

Jed decided to finish off Gary by humming a fastball by him on the lower outside corner of the plate. But a tired body wouldn't cooperate. The pitch didn't get down and out, but hung up over the middle, and it just didn't have all that much steam. Gary Chambers was waiting, and cracked the ball up the middle. The shortstop made a dive at the liner and knocked it down, but there was no play at first. It was an infield single.

"So that's Ohio's finest?" Gary needled from first base.

Jed acted like he was ignoring the runner and seemed to concentrate on getting the sign from the catcher. In reality, he was counting Gary's steps away from the bag. *Come on, Chambers, just a couple more. Nobody, absolutely nobody, takes four steps on Jed Rivers. One more step, you turkey.*

The pick-off throw caught Gary Chambers by surprise. By the time he dove back toward the base, the ball was already in the first baseman's glove and the tag was easily made. It made the second time in just a short, few minutes that Jed Rivers had forced Gary into the dirt. This time he was out!

As the teams walked off the field at the end of practice, Coach Stevens called out, "Nice move, Rivers!"

That wasn't exactly a guarantee of a starting role on the first team—but for a tired Jed, it was definitely progress.

Jed was hoping for a little progress in restoring the relationship with Ginny, too, but he couldn't figure out how to begin. He was still debating the issue in his mind when his mom called him to dinner.

"Where's Catherine?" he questioned. "I still haven't seen her since I got home."

"Oh, she said she'd be late. She wanted to stop by Ginny's house. I think she's afraid to face you," his Mom sighed.

"Yeah. She did ask about moving back to Ohio and staying with Grandma," Jed's dad laughed.

"Any chance we will be moving back? I mean, with you needing a job and all?" Jed questioned.

"Well, I'm really not sure. I'd like to get something out here, but who knows? I'm not in the mood to pack up and move again. How about you?"

"You know, two days ago I was ready to move back. Now . . . well, I think there are some things I need to solve first. Like this deal with Ginny."

"That reminds me, I should call them and have them send Catherine home. Jed, what's Ginny's number?" his mother asked.

"Ginny Rinaldi's? How would I know?"

"No, Ginny Greenly's."

"Catherine is at Ginny Greenly's?" Jed almost jumped out of his chair.

"That's what I've been saying all evening."

"What's she doing there!"

"She felt bad about the messed-up instructions last night, so she went to straighten it out."

"She what? Oh, no! I'm doomed! Maybe I could go away to military school with T.J.," Jed moaned.

The front door banged open and Catherine flew into the room giving orders in her Lady Anne best.

"Mother, we have company at the front door. Dad, Mr. Greenly's here. Jed, I'm really sorry for being such a nerd last night. Come on folks, you don't want them to see our messed-up kitchen."

Jed, a little dazed by the confusion, walked with his parents to the front door and welcomed Ginny and her father into the room.

"Hi, Jed. I'm glad T.J.'s dad is safe. Sorry about all this confusion . . . it's kind of weird," Ginny started to explain.

"Jed, we all owe you a big apology," Mr. Greenly continued. "Now, I know I'm possessive of Ginny. I just love that girl so much I can't bear to think of sharing her attention with someone else. Maybe you'll understand someday. Anyway, when these suggestive letters began appearing at our door signed by 'J.R.,' well, I assumed. . . ."

Ginny broke back in. "We all assumed that it was you. I mean, you are the only J.R. we know."

"But then," Mr. Greenly continued, "little Catherine came over and put us on the right track. It must be some off-the-wall character trying to mess things up for you."

"Catherine straightened you out?"

"Yeah," Catherine beamed. "It was a snap. There's no way you could have written those letters."

"But . . . how?" Jed was still puzzled.

"Oh, Jed," Catherine continued, "you have to admit you write really funny. I mean, being left-handed and all, your words look like they are about to lay down and take a nap. All the words on those letters leaned the opposite direction. They were written by somebody right-handed."

"And you figured that out?" Jed smiled at his sister.

"Hey, good looks, intelligence . . . it runs in the family," she giggled. "And don't worry, I'll think of some way you can thank me."

It was about an hour later before the Greenly's left, and Jed and his family resumed dinner. It had been a profitable time. Not only had the dilemma about the letters been solved, but Jed had been invited to go with Ginny and her family down to Tucson on Saturday.

After dinner Jed searched the want ads, half looking for a part-time job, half looking for an opening for his father. A phone call from T.J. ended the search.

"Jed? Hey, dude, I'm headin' over your way. Are you still awake?"

"Yeah . . . great! Hey, listen, T.J., I've got one mondo favor to ask of you."

"You got it. Do you still want me to try to talk to Ginny?"

"No, I need you to talk to Catherine."

"Who?"

"My little sister, Catherine. Let me explain. . . ." Jed filled T.J. in on what happened with Ginny Greenly and her father. In less than a half hour, T.J. was at the front door of the Rivers' home. Jed watched from the hall as Catherine answered the door.

"Oh . . . Hi!" Catherine stuttered.

"Excuse me, ma'am. I'm T.J. Bell. I'm a friend of your little brother's."

"My what?" Catherine shook her head.

"I'm a friend of Jed's. I didn't know he had an older sister."

"Oh, Jed. Yeah. Well . . . actually, I'm not older than Jed. Really, I'm younger . . . you know, a little."

"Hey, T.J.," Jed joined in with a smile, "come in. I see you met my sister, Catherine."

"Jed, you didn't tell me about some foxy-looking sister," T.J. added. "Do you mind if I call you Cathy?"

"She hates to be called . . . " Jed began.

"Jed!" Catherine stomped. "Don't interrupt. I'd love to have you call me Cathy."

"You wouldn't happen to have plans to be in New Mexico in May, would you?" T.J. asked.

"No," Catherine responded with wide eyes. "Why?"

"Oh, we have this big party at the end of the term, and it would be quite a privilege to have you as my date."

"It would? Oh, no! I can't. I mean . . . you know, my father won't let me date until I'm 16."

"Well, you're going to break my heart," T.J. continued. "Will you promise to save me that first date, when you turn 16?"

"Really?" Catherine's mouth dropped open.

"I mean it." T.J. took Catherine's hand and ␣ squeeze.

She floated off to her room mutterin␣ about having to call Ginny Rinaldi.

T.J. turned back to Jed. "All right␣ even."

"Even? Don't you think you we␣ board?" Jed laughed.

"She's a neat girl."

"Well, Texas Jack Bell, thanks. You made her day, week, and year."

"Hey, Jedediah Wilson Rivers, that's what good friends are for."

The Lucky Shirt

Not until Catherine called to him a third time did Jed realize that he had been staring at the bathroom mirror for an inordinate length of time.

It wasn't that he disliked what he viewed.

Rather, it was just one of those times that what he looked like on the outside needed to stop and say "hello" to what he looked like on the inside. For weeks Jed had been so busy he didn't have much time to consider how he looked.

Baseball tournaments, Biology projects, and a weekend job pushed him through the month without much time to reflect.

But this morning . . . Jed figured his dark brown hair was neat, his straight teeth glistened, his blue eyes looked rested, his upper body felt lean and muscular, and that knock-out smile was in place. He pushed open the door and turned toward his bedroom.

"It's all yours, Cath. . . . "

"Oh, man . . . you aren't going to wear that shirt, are you?" his sister nagged.

"What?" Jed snapped back to real life. "Oh, sure. . . I guess. Is there something wrong?"

"Well, it makes you look like a thirteen-year-old nerd," Catherine added. "Of course, who am I to say?" She disappeared behind the closed bathroom door.

Jed stepped into his sister's room and glanced at her full-length mirror.

Jeans, tennies, bright floral print shirt. . . . He slipped on his dark glasses. *What's she talking about?*

The blender roared as he entered the kitchen where his mother prepared breakfast. "Jed, did you know that Mr. Bell offered your father a job?"

"T.J.'s dad? Doing what?"

"Manager of the Oilfield Tool Division, or something like that," Mrs. Rivers added as she poured the contents of the blender onto a hot grill. "He hasn't decided to take it, but it's a very good offer."

"Man, that's an answer to prayer," Jed nodded as he searched the sports page for baseball scores. "So why is Dad hesitating?"

"Well . . . Jed, that shirt looks sloppy . . . uh, he wants to make sure that Mr. Bell really wants him to do the job. He doesn't want an offer just because you and T.J. are friends."

"It looks sloppy?"

"Oh, honey, maybe it's just me."

Mr. Rivers had a hammer in his hand as he entered the room. "What's just you? Morning, Jed. . . . My word, where did you get that shirt? It looks like some curtains left over from the sixties."

"All right! I know everyone hates this shirt. Well, I like it. Mind if I eat breakfast out on the patio?"

Jed met Ginny at the 43rd Avenue signal.

"Whoa, turn out the lights!" Ginny laughed.

Jed stared right at the sparkle in Ginny's green eyes. "What?" he stammered.

"That is one bright shirt!"

"Man, this is incredible. . . . Everybody hates this shirt. What's the matter with the world anyway? Why can't a guy just wear what he wants? I don't see why. . . ."

"OK . . . I can see you're a tad sensitive," Ginny teased. "It's just so different from what the conservative dressing Jed Rivers normally wears."

"Look, maybe it's just part of my wild side," he suggested.

"It's wild all right," Ginny mumbled.

"What?"

"I said, 'Does Jed Rivers really have a wild side?' "

Jed looked up and down the street, then in a low tone mimicked, "Did I ever tell you just why I got run out of Ohio?"

"Run out? I didn't know you were run out."

"Oh, sure," Jed joked. "It's a well-kept secret."

"Let's see, you did something really bizarre. . . . Well, did you put peanut butter on your popcorn, or what?" she prodded.

"What's bizarre about that?" Jed feigned seriousness. "Add a little salsa and you have a meal."

"OK, Rivers, that's gross. Why were you run out of Idaho?"

"Not Idaho . . . Ohio. You see, I once cleverly disguised all of the old blackboard erasers to look like 'Tuna Surprise' casserole at the school cafeteria."

"And?"

"And, they ate it for six months before anyone could tell the difference! Listen, you really don't like the shirt?"

"Hey, Rivers!"

Jed and Ginny turned around to see Mark Whitney walking up from behind.

67

"Rivers, did you get the license number of that truck?"

"Truck?"

"The one that ran over you, man. He completely ruined your shirt."

"This is going to be a long day," Jed sighed. "Look, both of you, this is my lucky shirt."

"You've worn it before?" Ginny giggled.

"You'll be lucky to make it through the day," Mark added.

Jed spent most of the morning at school defending his shirt.

"Mr. Rivers?"

"Yes, Mrs. Brandersen?"

"Would you and your shirt mind sitting in the back of the class today? It is difficult to concentrate on the finer details of Hamlet while neon green, purple and orange palm trees sway in the second row."

Only baseball practice, wearing the required warm-up jersey, brought some relief.

"Rivers, get in there and throw your best stuff," Coach Stevens hollered. If you can blow 'em past these guys I'll give you a shot at the first team.

There are days when a guy stands on the mound and he knows, without any doubt, that he has the batters beat.

This was one of those days.

Jed called his own pitches, throwing them tight and inside, then down and out, mixing them with a big curve and an occasional change-up.

He didn't hear a word from Gary Chambers nor from any of the others. Finally, after a half-dozen batters, the coach called out, "For Pete's sake, Rivers, let them hit one once in a while. . . . You'll get the whole team demoralized. Rest that arm a bit. I don't want you worn out before you start that game next Tuesday against Mesa."

Alright! Jed clenched his left hand around the ball and pounded it in the air. *Man, it must be my lucky shirt!*

Ginny waited for him after practice, and they started the walk home.

"Then Coach Stevens says, 'Rivers, you're going to start the game against Mesa.' Is that great, or what?"

"I knew you could do it," Ginny added. "Of course, you'll be up against Spring Taylor."

"Who?"

"Spring Taylor, the hot-shot pitcher over at Mesa."

"Spring? That's a guy's name?"

"Oh, yeah. You've heard of Summer Taylor, he plays at State? Well. . . ."

"Let me guess—there are four brothers named Summer, Fall, Winter and Spring?" Jed laughed.

"Nope. Only two," Ginny offered. "But they say Spring is better than his brother already. I don't think he's lost a game for two years. Anyway, I'm sure you'll do fine."

"You want to walk through the mall before we head home?"

"Sure. Do you need to do some shopping? . . . Perhaps a new shirt?"

Jed stopped in his tracks, dropped his backpack full of books, and pretended to be angry. "Listen, Greenly, one more peep out of you and I'll yank off this shirt, rip it into shreds, and stomp it into the gutter. Do you understand!"

"Peep."

"That's it!"

"No, Jed . . . wait," Ginny pleaded. "Wait until you buy a new shirt, at least."

It took three stores before Jed found the shirt he wanted. It was a heavy, acid-washed, mottled grey T-shirt with a black silhouette of three Indian riders crossing some cactus-covered mountains.

"It really looks great . . . " Ginny announced. "Maybe you could just, you know, wear it home."

Jed left on the new shirt, cramming the bright print into the department store sack, stuffing it into the top of his backpack. Six minutes after walking Ginny home, he turned up his driveway and cut across to the back door.

Catherine and Ginny Rinaldi were in the back yard practicing handstands.

"Hi, Jed!" Ginny R. called out. "Nice shirt."

Catherine collapsed on the lawn and looked up. "Jed? Hey, what happened to that Las Vegas billboard you had on this morning?"

"Everybody at school was so jealous of my lucky shirt," Jed laughed, "that I had to take it off, just to be fair."

"I'm sure it looked good on you," Ginny R. nodded.

"Actually, Ginny, he looked like a jerk . . . a real. . . . "

Jed didn't hear the rest of the sentence. He was already inside the house reporting to his dad what had happened during baseball practice.

Nothing more was said about the bright print shirt, but Jed left it wadded up in the sack inside his backpack all week long.

It was a good week.

On Tuesday, he bench pressed 202 pounds for the first time.

On Wednesday, he got a 98 on the pop quiz in Biology.

On Thursday, Ginny Rinaldi got laryngitis.

On Friday, T.J. called.

"Hey, hombre . . . qué pasé?"

"T.J.? Where are you?"

"In the hallowed halls of the New Mexico Military Academy, where else?"

"Hallowed halls?"

"Actually, I'm out by the horse barn. Anyway, I heard your dad is going to work for Bell Petroleum."

"Yeah, he decided to take the job. I hope that doesn't complicate things. I mean, I don't have a great record getting along with his bosses' sons."

"No problemo. . . . Besides, he'll be working specifically for Mr. DeLong. He's a good guy, almost like an uncle to me. Dad says your dad is just the one he's been looking for. So, what's new on the Salt River?"

"Hey, get this." Jed explained, "I'm starting the game against Mesa on Tuesday."

"No kidding? That's great! Of course that means you go against. . . ."

"Yeah, yeah, I know—Spring Taylor, right?"

"You've got it. Man, that dude is fast."

"Yeah, so I've heard." Jed leaned back against the wall. "OK, T.J., give me everything you know about Spring Taylor." Twelve minutes later Jed hung up the phone.

Spending a Friday night working at a service station at the Thunderbird Road exit of I-17 North was not Jed's idea of a great evening. On the other hand, $6.25 an hour did make up for some of the sacrifice.

About 7:05 p.m. a couple of blue vans marked "Mesa High School" pulled up to the self-service island. About two dozen guys piled out and swarmed around the pop machines.

Jed strolled over to the drivers who were busy filling both rigs.

"Evenin'. You don't happen to be the Mesa baseball team?" he asked in a casual tone.

"Sure are, son," the man in the blue shorts replied. "We're on our way home from Prescott."

"Oh, yeah? How'd you do up there?"

"Well, I'm mighty proud of the boys." He topped off the tank and replaced the nozzle in the pump. "Yeah, we whipped them pretty good. Mind you, Prescott has a strong team this year."

Jed shifted his weight from one foot to the other. "Well, what was the score?"

"Eh, I think it ended up 17-1, didn't it, Frank?"

The other man nodded, and the coach reached into his wallet for a credit card.

As Jed filled out the credit card information he continued the conversation.

"Who pitched for you?"

"Taylor."

"Spring Taylor?"

"Yeah."

"I've heard of him."

"You and every major league scout in the southwest."

Jed handed the man back his card.

"How about North West, what kind of team are they going to have this year?"

"Well, they've got a couple of big-time batters, and the right-handed kid, Chambers, who can pitch the ball. But I figure they don't have any depth. They could play us tight for a few innings, but sooner or later we'd bust loose."

Jed started to keep silent, then blurted out, "I hear they have a new left-hander that's pretty good."

"Oh yeah?" the coach asked. "Who's that?"

"Rivers. Jed Rivers," Jed offered.

"Never heard of him. You ever heard of him, Frank?"

"Nah, they haven't had a good left-hander at North West in ten or twelve years," Frank added.

As the team filed back into the vans, Jed asked, "Say, which one is Spring Taylor?"

"The big guy . . . with the hat on backwards."

Jed looked up to see a guy well over six feet tall.

"How tall is he?"

"Six feet six, 220 pounds of muscle and brains. Best kid I've ever coached."

Jed watched carefully as Taylor climbed up into the front bucket seat.

The guy's a mountain! Jed gulped.

Baseball suddenly became a depressing subject.

Fortunately, it was a busy evening and left little time for idle thought.

About 9:15 a man in a tattered business suit pushed a small sedan up to the station's curb. Jed went out to help him push the car.

"Run out of gas?" he asked the man.

"Oh. Yes. It's very embarrassing. I'm on my way to some meetings down in Nogales, and I just didn't pay attention to the gas gauge."

"You want regular or unleaded?" Jed puffed as he slowed the car down in front of the pumps.

"Uh, well . . . unleaded. But, listen . . . son, do you believe in God?"

"Huh?"

"I said, 'Do you believe in God?' "

Jed regained his thoughts. "Oh, yeah, I sure do. But, eh, what's that got to do with your gas?"

The man looked in his side mirror and straightened his tie, then brushing off his dusty sleeves he looked Jed right in the eyes. "You see, I accidently left my wallet back at the motel in Flagstaff. And I've ended up here in Phoenix without a dime. I've got friends down in Nogales, and so . . . well, I just need a little gas to get on down the road. I'll be speaking at some churches down there so everything will be fine. As I was considering my predicament out on the highway, I just felt led to come into this station and ask if you believed in God. I believe the Lord wants you to lend me a tank of gas."

Jed looked the man over carefully.

"The Lord wants me to lend you gas?"

"I believe so."

"Eh, how do you lend gas?"

"Well, what I mean is . . . when the meetings are through down in Nogales, I'll be driving right back through Phoenix—so I'll just stop and pay you back. It won't be more than a few days."

Jed searched around for his boss, and then remembered that he had left early.

"Don't you have any family or friends in Phoenix that can help you?"

"Oh, I'm afraid not. You see, I'm from Utah. Up around Ogden. I don't know anyone in Phoenix."

"I'm sorry, but I just can't give away gas."

"Oh, I didn't want you to jeopardize your job. I thought you could just pay for it yourself," the man suggested.

"Me? Use my own money?" Jed stammered.

The man looked down at his watch? "Oh . . . my, it is late. Yes, yes, just use your own money and I'll be on my way. You did say you were a believer, correct?"

"Well, yeah. It seems funny that the Lord told you to pull in here for free gas, but He didn't mention a thing about it to me."

"Now, I didn't say free gas. I will pay you back. I believe $20 worth will get me to Nogales—don't you think so?"

He reached for the nozzle on the pump. Jed blocked his hand.

As he did that, Jed heard a honk at the full service pump. He turned to see a blue Mustang convertible, with the soft top pulled up tight, waiting for attention.

"Mister, you have to pay for the gas. I've got other customers."

"Son, are you sure of your commitment to the Lord?"

"Yes, sir, I am. But no money—no gas."

Jed walked up to the Mustang and noticed an older lady behind the wheel. By the time he checked her oil, water, tires, washed the windshield and filled the tank with gas, he had forgotten about the man in the sedan.

"Thank you, young man." The lady counted out the exact change.

"Oh, sure. Nice car you have." Jed pointed at the Mustang.

"It belongs to Herald. I don't drive it much."

"Who's Herald?"

"My husband. He used to drive this little number all over the state."

"He doesn't drive much now?" Jed asked.

"Well, now, I couldn't tell you that. Herald passed away two years ago come September. I have my Lincoln, but every few weeks I drive the Mustang, just to keep it in shape."

Jed looked again at the car. "Do you ever think about selling it?"

"Are you interested in buying it?" she asked.

"Oh, yes, ma'am." Then he caught himself, "But—really, I won't have the money until later in the year. I'm saving up for a car."

"Well," she said, "I'd have to have $1,900 for it."

"$1,900?" Jed stammered.

"Oh, I know it needs some work, but that's what Herald paid for it, used, back in 1969. I need to get my money back."

"Ma'am, would you mind writing your phone number on the back of this receipt. I'd like to call you up later this summer and see if the car is still for sale."

"I won't be getting a bunch of wild phone calls now, will I?" she quizzed. "A girl has to watch out who has her number."

"Ma'am, I guarantee that I will not let anyone even see this number." Jed wrote "great buy on a '65 Mustang" on the receipt and stuck it carefully into the back of his wallet.

When he remembered the man out front, he spun around to see the sedan drive out of the station and head up to the freeway entrance.

"Hey! How'd you get that. . . ." Jed ran to the pump and found a note folded under the handle.

"I didn't want to bother you further. Please pay your boss $20 for my gas, and your books will be balanced. I will repay you when I return. The Lord bless you. Norris N. Norton."

"Oh, man!" Jed kicked the pump.

When Jed finally got home, about 10:20 p.m., the only thing he had in his wallet was an old lady's phone number, and an I.O.U. from Norton.

One Of A Kind

"I would have called the police!" Catherine wailed when Jed related the story of the man in the sedan to his family the next day.

"Yeah, well, it's just . . . you know. What if the Lord did tell him to come into the station? I mean, aren't we suppose to give when someone asks?"

"Sure. Listen, Jed, I'd like for you to give me all the money you make at the station from now on," Catherine whined.

"Catherine! Jed might be right," his mother added. "You can't give away all your money, but you certainly have to be open to the Lord's leading."

"Anyway, I didn't have any choice. Everything's been going great all week until then. Did I tell you about the lady who wants to sell the Mustang?"

"About a hundred times," Catherine reported as she traipsed off to her room.

"Well, no matter what, I say this has been one great week! Maybe it's because I wore my lucky shirt," Jed announced, then banged out the front door and headed for work.

Jed's great week ended at 4:45 p.m. that afternoon. That's when Mr. Schilling called all his crew together and announced he was closing the service station. By May 15th they would all be unemployed.

79

On Sunday, he got to Sunday school early and found out from Daffy that Ginny had a horrible stomach flu and was home sick in bed. Mrs. Greenly told Jed not to bother calling—Ginny was way too sick even to talk.

Monday morning, between classes, Mark Whitney grabbed Jed next to the lockers.

"Hey, Rivers! Have you still got that wild shirt you wore the other day?"

"Eh, yeah, why?"

"Well, if I were you, I'd hide it. . . . Look at this!"

Mark shoved a newspaper at Jed. On the cover was a story about a Scottsdale supermarket robbery. A video camera had captured the thief on film—and besides wearing a nylon stocking over his head, he had on a bright-colored, Hawaiian print shirt identical to Jed's.

"That's my shirt!"

"I hope not," Mark added. "We need you to pitch that game tomorrow."

Jed dug through his backpack but couldn't find the sack with the print shirt. After baseball practice he hurried home to rummage through his closet.

"Catherine! Catherine, have you seen my lucky shirt?"

"You're what?"

"I mean, that Hawaiian shirt that was so popular last week. Have you seen it?"

"Yeah. Your troubles are over, big brother. I sold it."

"You what?"

"I sold it for twenty-five cents at the junior high yard sale on Saturday. Mother said I could have your old clothes."

"You did what? A yard sale? Where? When? To whom?"

"What's the matter, anyway? Jed, it really did look pitiful."

"Who did you sell it to?"

"Some guy in a yellow truck . . . I don't remember."

"Well, you'd better try to remember. Somebody wearing that shirt held up a supermarket in Scottsdale!"

"It doesn't surprise me. I think it's a crime just to wear that shirt."

For thirty minutes before Tuesday's big game with Mesa, Jed tried to psyche himself up. He was determined to think about a blazing fastball, but his mind kept coming back to Norris N. Norton taking off with twenty buck's worth of gas. Then he tried to outthink Spring Taylor, but his mind drifted back to closing the station and losing his job.

When he tried to stretch out, down by the bull pen, he thought about Ginny, still at home, sick. And when he jogged out to center field and back with the rest of the team, his mind was on some creep running around town robbing stores and wearing his lucky shirt.

He was standing on the sidelines when the stupidity of the whole process finally hit him.

"Lucky shirt! Man, Lord, what am I thinking? I know You're in charge . . . it's just . . . You know, a little game. Help me, Lord, just to concentrate on one pitch at a time."

Seven innings and a shower later, Jed left the locker room and searched for his dad among the crowd that was still left in the parking lot.

"Rivers!"

Jed turned to see the towering Spring Taylor coming his way.

"Listen, that was a great game you pitched, Rivers."

"Call me Jed. Thanks. It was one of the best I ever pitched . . . and lost."

"I'm not bragging, but you lose to Mesa one-zip, and it's like beating every other team in the state. Nobody's come that close in three years. I usually coast in after the fourth or fifth inning. Man, you had me sweating until the last pitch."

Jed turned and walked with Spring Taylor toward the Mesa vans. "You're the one that had a great game. We only got four hits."

"Sure, but everybody knows I'm a great pitcher," Taylor said without any sign of emotion. "What we didn't know was how good Jed Rivers is. But we do now. See you next time."

"Hey, champ . . . great game."

Jed turned to see his dad walking up.

"Yeah, you know what's funny, Dad. I've never felt so good about losing. I mean, I just know I pushed myself to the limit, and that's all I can do. You know what I mean?"

"You've got it, kid. That's what life's all about, isn't it? We push ourselves to the limit of the talent, brains, projects that the Lord gives us . . . then we relax and enjoy the outcome."

"You know, Dad, we could have beat them. Man, we gave Mesa the scare of their lives. Anyway, it's a great way to start the season. If I can keep that attitude I'll have a good year."

"And you'll have a lot of wins," his dad added.

Ginny called about the time he walked into the house after the game.

"Hey, champ, I heard you almost slayed Goliath," she chirped.

"Ginny! Are you feeling all right?"

"Lots better, thanks. Jed, did you see the news tonight?"

"Nah, I just walked in."

"Well, there's a story about a guy who held up a supermarket over in Glendale, and he was wearing a shirt that sounded identical to yours—you know, that ... weird one?"

"Weird? Yeah, I heard about that. But I thought it was a market over in Scottsdale."

"That was Sunday. . . . This is the same guy, same shirt, but a different store," Ginny added.

"You want to hear something bizarre? Catherine took my shirt to a yard sale and sold it for a quarter on Saturday. Ginny, I think that guy really is wearing my shirt!"

"You're kidding!"

"No. Think about it. How many of those shirts can there be around. This missionary friend of ours down in Jamaica sent it to my dad, but he would never wear it."

"Smart man."

"Anyway ... I know it's my shirt. But Catherine said she can't remember anything about the guy who bought it—except that he drove a little yellow pickup ... maybe?"

"Maybe?"

"Yeah, that's exactly what the police said when Catherine reported the sale. Anyway, it's sad to see a perfectly decent shirt turn to a life of crime. Who knows what it could have been if it would have had a decent home, and someone who loved it."

"Oh croak it, Rivers. That shirt was born criminal. Only a deranged mind would wear it."

"Yeah, well . . . thanks. Hey, did you hear that Mr. Schilling is closing down the service station on the 15th of May?"

"No. When did he tell you that?"

"On Saturday, but you were too sick to talk to. I've really missed you. You're my favorite person to talk to, especially when T.J.'s gone to New Mexico."

"When's your next game?" Ginny quizzed.

"I'll have about one a week. I hope they aren't all as hard as Mesa."

"Well, I don't intend on missing any of the others," Ginny added.

She didn't.

Once each week Jed started a game for North West High. Once a week he won a game for North West High. And, once a week the Flower Blossom Shirt Bandit (as he was known in the newspapers) robbed another store.

By the middle of May, the service station closed down and Jed was out of work. By May 20th, baseball season was over, and Jed ended up 8-1 with an E.R.A. of 1.98. On May 25th, the Flower Blossom Bandit robbed his 10th store in southern Arizona, and there was a $2,500.00 reward for any information that led to his arrest. On May 28th, T.J. finished up at the New Mexico Academy and made his way back to Phoenix.

On T.J.'s first Friday night back in town, he, Jed, and Ginny piled into his pickup and headed down to Pearl's.

"So, my main man, Jed Rivers, finished with a great season! It doesn't surprise me a bit," T.J. boasted.

"Me either," Ginny added. "Next year, he'll be 9-0."

"Yeah, maybe. But maybe next year all those guys will know how much curve Rivers has, and be waiting to cream that thing. If I don't pick up a little more speed, I'll be in trouble."

"And he's so modest, T.J."

"Tell T.J. what Gary Chambers said to you."

"Chambers is speaking to you again?"

"Yeah, after my eighth win he walked over and said, 'Nice game. You know, Rivers, you're one of the luckiest pitchers I've ever seen.' "

T.J. pulled into the back lot at Pearl's and hopped out of the truck. "Lucky? Well, I guess that's about the best Gary could do. Did you find a job yet?"

"Not me," Jed shrugged. "Ginny's going to work at the Pie Palace, but I still need something. I've got to save up this summer. Hey, did I tell you about that Mustang?"

T.J. grabbed Jed around the shoulders. "Every time you called you talked about that car, Rivers! I wish you'd hurry up and buy it, so I don't have to listen to you whine."

"I'm all for that. You know of any openings?" Jed quizzed.

"Not me. I'm headed for four weeks in Mexico with my dad. But if I were looking for a job, I'd try looking in Scottsdale. The wages are better."

"Better than Paradise Valley?"

"Hey, nobody works for wages in Paradise Valley," T.J. laughed.

Well, let's go to Scottsdale and look around," Jed suggested.

"Right now? Everything will be closed," Ginny offered.

"Sure, but we can nose around, right?"

"You got it," T.J. added. "I'm just the driver."

They were on McDowell Road, going east, just past 32nd Street when Jed suddenly shouted.

"Hey! Look up there! There's my shirt!"

"Your what?" T.J. asked.

"You heard about these market robberies?" Ginny explained. "Well, Jed is convinced the guy is wearing one of his old shirts that Catherine sold at a yard sale."

Jed waved his hands as he talked. "Really, look! It's a little yellow pickup, just like Catherine said. Let's follow him!"

"A criminal? You're kidding," Ginny moaned.

"Yeah. Look, there's a $2,500 reward, and we could split it three ways. What do you say?"

"I say, let's follow the guy as long as he's on this street headed for Scottsdale," T.J. proposed.

Just past the peaks in Papago Park, the yellow pickup made a sharp right turn and zipped down a narrow, paved road through a stand of yucca. T.J. pulled off, and the trio watched the tail lights disappear around a bend in the road.

"Hey, what's down there, a big store, or a mall or something?" Jed asked.

"Hardly," T.J. informed. "That's the Phoenix Botanical Gardens. You know, where they have those desert plants and stuff."

"He's going to rob a botanical garden?" Jed pondered.

"Maybe he's not a thief at all," Ginny cautioned.

"Look, I know my shirt when I see it, and that was my shirt. T.J. pull down that road after him."

When they reached the big, empty parking lot of the now closed Botanical Gardens, Jed spotted the yellow truck parked behind one of the smaller buildings.

"Kill the lights! Let's park it here and see what happens," Jed suggested.

"This is a little too dramatic for me," Ginny added. "Let's go to Scottsdale."

"Nah," T.J. laughed, "I've never played 'follow that shirt' before."

"Yeah, you guys laugh, but when they start giving out reward money . . . you'll be in line just like me. Let's walk over there and peek into that window with the light on."

"Let's go to Scottsdale," Ginny insisted.

"Well, if we get caught, I'll tell the guy we were looking for a bloom from a rare night-blooming cactus," T.J. offered.

Jed led the way. "Do they really do that? Do they bloom in the dark?"

"That's what they tell me. Hey, look at that! The guy's in there, ripping off a handful of cash," T.J. whispered.

Still a good distance from the building, Jed and Ginny climbed on a boulder and peaked through the window.

"Man, he's filing the cash box!"

"It looks like he's counting it to me," Ginny reported.

"Yeah, he wants to know how much he is getting," Jed explained.

Ginny started to climb down. "Nobody counts their money during a crime, do they? I mean, don't they always wait until they get away before they count it?"

"Obviously, not tonight. Man, we've caught him red-handed. Is there a pay phone around here?" Jed asked.

"Over near the entrance to the parking lot," T.J. pointed in the shadows.

"Ginny, go call the police. Tell them we've caught the Flower Blossom Shirt Bandit in the act, but they'll have to hurry," Jed barked the orders in a low voice.

Ginny trotted off across the asphalt while T.J. and Jed scooted closer to the window for a better look.

"Man," T.J. whispered, "what will we do if this dude starts to leave?"

"We'll just have to think of something. Look. He's putting the money in a bag."

"Yeah, it's a bank deposit bag."

"A what?"

T.J. turned to Jed, "You know, one of those night deposit bags like a business would use."

"Why would he want to steal that?"

"Fellas?" Ginny was calling across the parking lot. "Hey, where are you guys?"

"Shh! Ginny, keep it down!" Jed cautioned.

She ignored his advice and talked in a normal tone. "Guys, hey look, I talked to the police."

"Yeah? What did they say?" T.J. still whispered.

"They said the Flower Blossom Bandit was arrested in Palm Springs yesterday, and he confessed to the whole thing. I guess it was in this morning's paper. I must have missed it."

"He what?" Jed groaned. "Then who's this guy?"

"Why don't you ask him? Here he comes." Ginny tried to smile at the guy in the bright flowered shirt. In the glow of the parking lot light, she could barely see his face.

"You kids looking for something?" the man asked.

"Uh, well . . ." Jed stammered. "Nice shirt."

"Hey, isn't this wild? I picked this up at a yard sale for two bits, but couldn't wear it until today. You know—all that scare about the Flower Blossom Bandit had people jumpy."

"Did you get it at Bonner Junior High?"

"Yeah . . . how did you know?"

Jed shifted his weight from one foot to the other and looked at his shoes. "Oh, it's . . . well, it used to be my shirt. My sister sold it there."

"And you want to buy it back?"

"No he doesn't," Ginny jumped in.

"Definitely not," T.J. added.

"Then why are you here? Are you looking for that summer job? Hey, I didn't think it went into the paper until tomorrow."

"Yes, sir, as a matter of fact I would very much like to have a job," Jed stammered. "Ginny and T.J. already have some things lined up, but I would like to work!"

"What's your name?"

"Jed Rivers."

"Well, Jed . . . can you be here at 6:00 a.m. on June 6th?"

"Yes, sir."

"You've got the position. I like a guy who will give up cruising on a Friday night just to look for a job."

"No kidding? Thanks, sir."

"Roger. Just call me Roger. Now I've got to get these receipts down to the bank. You can stop by any day and pick up some personal forms to fill out. . . .

Say, Jed, you don't have any more of these great shirts, do you?"

"No, sir. I mean, Roger. I think maybe that's sort of a one-of-a-kind shirt," Jed confessed.

The trio made their way back to Pearl's to celebrate Jed's new job. It was 11:21 p.m. when Jed got home. Catherine, blurry-eyed and bathrobed, met him at the door.

"Mom and Dad won't be home for another hour, I'm going to bed, this old movie is really boring."

"Hey, Cath, I got a summer job at the Botanical Gardens!"

"Jed, you don't know anything about boats!"

"Go to bed, Cath. . . . I'll tell you in the morning."

"Jed, Mr. Schilling brought you by that envelope. I guess some guy left it at the service station after it closed up."

Jed picked up the envelope and stared at four $5 bills inside. On the outside it read, "For the left-handed, blue-eyed kid. Thanks. Norris N. Norton."

"Norton? Norton! The guy who made me buy him some gas? Alright! He did pay me back! Man, is this my lucky day, or what?"

Jed spun around, but Catherine had disappeared down the hall toward her bedroom.

Thanks, Lord, Jed corrected. *I know it's not really luck.*

Cruising

Jed sat cross-legged on the kitchen floor, a bag of potato chips scrunched in his lap, with the telephone tucked between his ear and shoulder. His blue tank top, emblazoned with "Just Do It," revealed his tanned arms. He waited for Ginny's friendly greeting.

"Hey, you want to go for a cruise in *my* new car?" he blurted.

"You really bought it? The blue Mustang?" Ginny shrieked.

"Yep."

"So, what did you pay for it?"

"Uh, well, let's just say I spent everything I've been working day and night all summer to save."

"Oh, Jed, I'd love to go for a ride . . . but Mr. Cranston just called and Bev is sick, so he wants me to work tonight."

"Can I pick you up after work?"

"Sure, but it's Saturday, so I don't get off until 10:10. Remember?"

"I'll be there."

Jed jumped to his feet and poured the last bite of potato chips into his mouth when the back door flung open. Catherine grabbed his arm, scattering chip crumbs across the floor.

"Great work, freshman," Jed said, then handing her a broom.

She swiped at the crumbs. "Listen, Jed, what if I promised to take your turn with the chores every night for a month?"

"I can hardly wait to hear this." He opened the refrigerator door and searched for a Diet Coke.

Catherine stood on the first step of the footstool so that she was Jed's height. "All I want is a ride in your new car."

"A ride? That's it?" Jed questioned.

"Well, almost." Catherine wiggled her nose. "Here's the deal . . . you and one of your friends . . . say T.J. . . . and me and one of my friends . . . say Ginny Rinaldi . . . go for a ride in your Mustang tonight. What do you think?"

"And you'll do chores for a month?"

"You got it, big brother."

"Well, call Ginny R., and you two can ride with me down to the mall to buy some chrome cleaner." Jed headed for his room.

"Wait!" Catherine followed close behind. "There's just a little bit more. See, I figure we ought to ride up and down Central a few times with the top down. Then . . . well, we pull into Pearl's for a hamburger or something."

"Cruise Central? Me? With my little sister?"

"I'm 14, and I look old for my age."

"Says who?"

"T.J. . . . remember, he thought I was older than you."

"T.J. is in New Mexico!" Jed had a sudden urge to be an only child.

Catherine pulled a thick strand of long, brown hair across her face and wrinkled her nose as she replied, "Well, Ginny and I just saw him at Casa Luigi's."

"You must have just seen someone who looks like T.J."

Catherine took a deep breath and spun around sighing, "No one, I repeat, no one looks like T.J. Bell."

"I'm going to the mall. If you and Ginny R. want to ride along, be ready to go in ten minutes."

"Alright, I'll take it. But the chore deal is off."

Catherine hurried back into the kitchen to answer the persistent phone. Jed listened in.

Her brown eyes glistened as she began blurting out a conversation without waiting to hear who the caller was. "Listen, Ginny, Jed said it was OK and he'll be leaving in ten minutes. I'm going to wear my pink jeans and that blouse with the flowers . . . it makes me look mature. But I'm not sure if he's bringing a friend, it's the. . . ."

Jed's sister grew suddenly silent, then shrieked, "T.J.? You aren't Ginny? I thought you were . . . Oh no! I mean, sure." She turned to see her brother at the door. "Jed . . . it's T.J.! Tell him . . . you know . . . I forgot to take my medicine and I don't know what I'm doing." Catherine shoved the phone in Jed's hand and rushed out of the room.

"T.J.? What's up? How's New Mexico?"

"Hold on to your boots, cowboy . . . I'm still in town. Last night dad and I decided that I should stay home this year. So, all day today we were over at North West High getting things arranged."

"No kidding?" Jed ran his fingers through his tousled, brown hair. "You were at North West on a Saturday?"

"One of the advantages of having a dad who owns Bell Oil. Dad knows the Superintendent of Schools. What do you say, let's celebrate. I've got a pizza."

"And I've got a '65 Mustang convertible."
"You bought the car?"
"Yeah—high mileage, worn transmission and all."
"All right! I'll be right over."

The hood was up on the Mustang, and Jed was giving Ginny Rinaldi and Catherine a mechanical tour of the insides when T.J. arrived in his pickup. His sun glasses hung around his neck and he was wearing a western shirt with the sleeves rolled up. A large pizza box was being carried with one hand.

"Pizza delivery man! Anyone here order a jumbo Canadian bacon and pineapple . . . minus one piece?" T.J. quizzed.

"Pineapple?" Jed laughed. "That leaves Catherine out, she hates. . . ."

"Oh, I think it's about time I cultivated some new tastes," Catherine broke in, brushing her hair back out of her eyes. "Thanks, T.J."

Jed slammed the hood and strolled toward the driver's seat.

"The secret will be to keep it running until next summer, when I can make some money to fix it up. Whoa! Isn't this cozy? Sorry, gals, T.J. and I sit in the front."

Catherine moaned, "Jed! We can't both sit back here. We'd look like. . . ."

"Like little sisters?" Jed added.

After a brief blitz of the Metrocenter Mall, Jed, T.J., and the girls drove over to Central Avenue. The street and sidewalks teemed with teens celebrating the last Saturday night of summer vacation. Jed glanced off to the west. The setting sun slid behind distant desert peaks to cast a red glow in the sky. The time and temperature sign flashed "8:06, 83°F." The warm wind that whipped into the convertible added to his sense of contentment.

"Only in Arizona!" he shouted above the blast of the stereo.

They lapped Central several times before pulling into Pearl's Drive-In. With its U-shaped, canvas-covered parking, carhops who brought your food to the window, and the menus yellowed with age . . . Pearl's felt to Jed like a scene from an old movie. The excess parking area provided a display of the best-looking cars on the Avenue. Corvettes, Trans-Ams, hot rods, low-riders, and an occasional Ferrari posed, often with hood open and a small congregation of surrounding, enthusiastic fans.

Jed pulled in next to a familiar blue Jeep.

Mark Whitney hollered out, "Hey, T.J.! You and Rivers doing a little freshman orientation?"

"These charming ladies are members of the Russian Ballet," T.J. insisted.

"And the Cardinals are going to win the Superbowl," Mark jibed. "Hey, Jed, is that yours?"

"Yeah, I just bought it."

T.J. wandered inside the drive-in, and Jed followed. For the next hour or so, Jed, T.J., and a friend named Spud Curtis daydreamed about driving up to Pearl's in a brand new Lamborghini.

"There is no way on earth I could ever own such a car," Spud concluded.

"Hey, I'm lucky to have a Mustang fixer-upper," Jed added.

"Well, don't look at me," T.J. sighed. "My dad still drives an '86 Blazer. He hates sports cars."

"Well," Spud laughed, "as soon as I'm eighteen, I'm going to win the Arizona Lottery. Even got the winning numbers picked out."

Jed leaned his head back on the vinyl cushion, closed his blue eyes, and smiled. "I think I'll just discover gold."

T.J. sat straight up. "Hey! Did I ever tell you guys about the time my dad and I discovered gold?"

"Over in New Mexico, right?" Jed shot back.

"Yeah, in the San Andres mountains. My dad bought the place, and we haven't had time to go back."

Spud swooped down for one of Jed's french fries and almost shouted, "So, let's drop out of school and go prospecting. We could be rich by Christmas!"

"Nah," T.J. laughed. "But listen, if you guys wanted to go over and look around, we could do that on a long weekend."

Spud slammed down his chocolate shake. "No kidding?"

"Hey, no guarantees we'd find anything but snakes," T.J. added.

"That does it, I'm not going! Me and snakes just don't get along," Spud added as he stood to leave. "Listen, you guys think of some other way to make a fortune, I'm in. I've got to run. I promised my folks I'd be home by ten."

"And I've got to get the girls home so I can pick up Ginny." Jed scooted out of the booth behind Spud.

T.J. and Jed approached the Mustang from the rear, their cowboy boots clomping across the parking lot. Jed noticed a couple of freshmen boys leaning against the car talking to Catherine and Ginny R., who were now sitting in the front seats.

T.J. took the lead. "Say, ladies, would you mind giving the two of us a ride? Our Porsche is in the shop."

The two younger boys stepped back and stared.

Catherine pulled her sun glasses down to the end of her nose, inspecting Jed and T.J. "Sure, Honey," Catherine purred. "We were just about ready to leave. Would one of you dudes like to drive?"

Jed took the keys and Catherine scurried into the back seat with T.J.

All four watched as the two younger boys picked up their skateboards and loped on down Central Avenue.

Jed flipped the key over. Nothing happened. He rattled the key several times in the slot, then turned it over again. A clicking sound answered from under the hood.

"No, no, no . . . this isn't happening to me!" Jed fumed.

"Dead battery, my good man," T.J. shrugged. "We should have hitched rides with some other girls."

"Catherine! Did you have the radio on the whole time we were inside?" Jed barked.

"Well, not really. I mean, we had it on quite a while and then it sort of . . . you know, faded out. So I turned it off."

"Nothing to do but get out and push." T.J. climbed out of the back seat and walked to the front. "You want Cathy to steer while we push?"

"Cathy? She hates. . . ."

"Jed!" his sister shot back.

"Er, well, I'm sure 'Cathy' would rather push," Jed replied.

"Oh, great. You are going to humiliate us in front of the whole world?" Catherine wailed.

Jed purposely did not look around the parking lot as the others rolled the Mustang back out on the side street. There were some events in his life that he just wanted to forever remove from his mind. He knew that this was one of them.

"OK," he barked, "push me as hard as you can toward the corner and I'll pop it in gear."

"Aye, aye, Captain Kirk," T.J. saluted. "We're taking her up to warp speed."

The Mustang rolled quickly down the street. Jed slipped it into second, and let out on the clutch. With a horrible grind and snap of metal, the car lurched forward. The engine coughed, then started, and the Mustang rolled to a stop.

"What was that noise?" T.J. shouted.

"Well, at least it started." Catherine hurried to get in the car.

Jed didn't look up.

He didn't say a word.

He didn't smile.

He just wiggled the gear shift back and forth.

"This is not happening to me," he finally moaned.

T.J. quizzed, "Trouble with the transmission?"

"Trouble? There's no transmission left!" Jed slammed his hand on the dash.

"Is that serious?" Ginny Rinaldi probed.

The boys stared in disbelief.

T.J. spoke first. "Listen, there's Mark. I'll catch a ride and bring back my pickup to tow you home."

"T.J., tell my Dad what happened . . . and ask him or Mom to go by and give Ginny Greenly a ride home from work. She'll be waiting for me."

"Right. See you in a few minutes, old buddy."

It was 34 minutes and 20 seconds before help came. Jed stared at his watch most of the time and kept wondering if his car was really worth a whole summer's work at the Phoenix Botanical Gardens. Meanwhile, Catherine and Ginny R. crouched down low in the cramped back seat.

Catherine finally broke the silence." Hey, it's Dad!"

Jed bounded out of the car. "Well, isn't this great? Listen, I'm really sorry to get you out. I thought T.J. was...."

Jed's dad reached in and wiggled the gear shift lever of the Mustang, then walked back to pull a tow chain out of the trunk of his car. "I sent T.J. to take your Ginny home. I figured you might need my help on this one."

Swinging under his car, Jed hooked the chain securely. "Thanks, Dad. Say, do you think there's any guarantee on this transmission?"

"Not a chance," Mr. Rivers nodded.

"And I don't suppose I could borrow some money to fix it?"

"I'm afraid you'll have to park this little beauty until you've saved up enough for repairs. Let's take it slow going home—and remember, I'm counting on your brakes to stop both of us."

"Right."

Mr. Rivers turned to the girls. "You two want to ride with me, or with Jed?"

Catherine scrambled to her father's car.

"Oh, I'll ride with Jed," Ginny R. began.

"You will *both* ride with Dad!" Jed ordered.

Jed listened to the clock in the entry hall strike eleven as he waited for his dad and Catherine to return from taking Ginny Rinaldi home. He flopped in a chair and tapped his fingers on the end table as he relived every embarrassing moment. Then, he leaped out of his depression at the sound of the telephone. Mr. Greenly's unmistakable voice boomed through the air.

"Rivers, I thought you were bringing my little Ginny home tonight?"

"Oh, yeah. Er, sir . . . the transmission on my car went out, and while Dad was towing me home, I . . . I mean, my dad sent T.J. to give Ginny a ride. They may be a little late, but it's my fault."

"The Bell kid? He's still in town, is he?"

"Yes, sir. He's going to North West this year."

"Is that right? What a break! Did you ever see that lad play football?"

"Er, no . . . not in a game or anything."

"He'll make starting quarterback, wait and see. I imagine that Ginny was really happy to hear the news. If she's with T.J. Bell, there's nothing to worry about. Right?"

Jed's thoughts began to wander to T.J. and Ginny in his friend's maroon pickup. *Will she sit next to the window?*

"Mr. Greenly? If it's alright with you, could you have Ginny call me for just a minute when she gets home. I want to know everything is OK?"

"Will do, son."

Jed woke up at 4:00 a.m., still sitting in the recliner in the living room, waiting for Ginny to call. He trudged off to his room and plopped down on top of the bed—but he couldn't sleep.

T.J. and Ginny.

Ginny and T.J.

His thoughts worried him.

His inability to think of anything else troubled him even more.

On the way to church he thumbed through his Bible, but stared out the car window at the passing buildings. *Lord, how come I feel uneasy about T.J. going to school in Phoenix? I mean, I had the whole year figured out with me and Ginny, and the Mustang. But now. . . .*

Jed hesitated as he pushed into the youth building. Daffy grabbed his arm and spun him around.

"Hey, did you hear the good news? T.J. is going to stay in Phoenix and go to North West!"

"Yeah," Jed shrugged. "Where is he?"

"He's up there in front with your Ginny," Daffy smiled. "With his turquoise shirt, and her shiny turquoise dress, they make a striking couple, don't you think?"

Jed felt like the transmission in his stomach had just ground to a halt. *Lord, I told You this was going to happen.*

The Right Chemistry

Jed couldn't imagine a more miserable first day of school. The computer fouled up and had him registered for Freshman English. He forgot his wallet and had to skip lunch. His Mustang was parked in the driveway with the transmission ground to bits. T.J. Bell was all anyone at high school wanted to talk about. And Ginny ignored him because of how he had acted on Sunday.

A guy's junior year just shouldn't start out this way, he reasoned with himself.

Jed sprawled in sixth period Chemistry class, staring at an overhead screen full of symbols and abbreviations as other students straggled into the room.

"Hi! I didn't see you at lunch." Jed turned to see Ginny plop down at the desk next to his.

"Yeah . . . well, I was in the library."

"On the first day of school?"

"Look, I was in the library. OK? Anyway, you looked busy." Jed glanced at Ginny and then returned his gaze to the screen.

"Not really." She smoothed down the only rumpled strand of her curly, brown hair. "Oh, T.J. came over and had lunch with me."

"Anyway, I figured you weren't speaking to me," Jed added. He noticed that she was wearing his

103

favorite teal green blouse. *Oh sure, she would wear that.*

"Yeah, well I shouldn't . . . I mean, sometimes you can act like such a jerk," Ginny whispered as the teacher greeted the class.

"Yeah, there are times you remind me of some airhead cheerleader." *I didn't say that, did I?*

"Jed, that's not fair!"

"Just forget it. Where's T.J.? Doesn't he have to take Chemistry with the rest of us mortals?"

"Oh, he took it a couple of years ago and got an 'A'."

"You've become an expert on T.J. Bell," Jed snapped.

"Hey, I've known T.J. for years . . . remember? Phoenix is our home."

"Yeah, and I'm still the outsider."

"That's not what I. . . ." Ginny's voice trailed off as the teacher began her lecture.

Jed didn't follow the opening remarks. His mind raced through the past two days. *Lord, how come, when I get uptight, I say such dumb things? Next time I'm going to smile and not say a word, that way I won't make things worse.*

Jed kept glancing at Ginny. Her incredible smile was absent, and he knew he was the reason for it. *This could be a long year* he sighed as he ran his hand through his dark brown hair.

He was only half paying attention when Mrs. Johnson divided the class into lab partners. Absent mindedly he scribbled Ginny's name down in his chemistry book.

"Lab partners?" He looked over at Ginny, but she had gone up front to talk to the teacher. When she returned she shrugged. "We can't change partners until after the first lab session."

When the class dismissed, everyone hurried out of the classroom, but Jed stayed in his seat, staring at the chemical element chart.

"It's amazing, isn't it, Jed?" Mrs. Johnson broke into his daydreams.

"Huh? What? Oh . . . the chart! Yes, ma'am. I guess class is over. Well, I, er . . . good-bye, Mrs. Johnson."

Jed grabbed some books out of his locker, jammed them into his backpack, and turned toward home.

"Hey Jed!" It was his sister Catherine's piercing voice.

"Jed wait!" She was gasping to catch her breath when she caught up. "Listen, high school is great. Man, I think I was born to be in high school, know what I mean?"

"Not really."

"Listen, you won't believe this . . . Brad Herndon asked me for a date!"

"Brad who?"

"Brad Herndon. He's a sophomore and has just moved here from San Diego. He already has his driver's license."

"A date? Dad won't let you go on a date." Jed looked Catherine up and down. *It's funny,* he thought, *Catherine never really looks like a girl . . . she just looks like a sister.*

"Well, yeah. But I'm going to talk to Mom and Dad. I mean, maybe once they meet Brad they'll change their minds. Jed, he is so . . . so . . . so, you know, 'just right'."

"You can tell that in one day?"

"Yep. You see, we have two classes together, and at lunch he came by where I was sitting and said, 'Hi! Can we get together and talk sometime?' And I said,

'Sure.' Then he said, 'What about Friday, at 7:00?' And I said, 'Sure.' Then he said, 'I'll pick you up in my Camaro and you can show me around Phoenix.' And I said. . . ."

"Let me guess," Jed broke in, "and you said, 'Sure.' "

Yeah. Isn't high school great! Yesterday I was just a kid, but today . . . I'm a woman."

"Have you got a barf bag? This sounds like some soap opera. You know for a fact that Dad won't let you go."

"He's just got to," Catherine pleaded. "This could be the most important week in my entire life. You understand, don't you, Jed? Some events just feel like they are going to be turning points. This is big, Jed. I can tell that this is really big."

Catherine clutched her books and tried to skip and catch up with Jed. "Come on, big brother, slow down!"

Jed shoved his free hand into the back pocket of his blue jeans and turned around to wait for his sister.

"Thanks. Listen, Jed, did you ever get that mess with your Ginny and T.J. straightened out?"

"Uh . . . not yet," Jed stammered.

"Well," Catherine continued, "did you talk to Ginny?"

"Yeah, I talked to her."

"And it's all cleared-up?"

"I don't want to talk about it."

"Hey, I can go fix it up for you again," Catherine offered.

"I don't want to talk about it."

"Look, lots of girls want to go out with you." Catherine sounded cheerful. "Take Ginny Rinaldi, for instance.

"Catherine, I do not want to talk about it!"

Jed turned up the street leaving Catherine, once again, running to keep up.

That night, after supper, Jed answered the phone.

"Hey, Ohio Slim, this is T.J., and I think we've got some talking to do."

Jed remained aloof, "Oh?"

"Yeah. Ginny said you were still steamed about that ride we took Saturday night."

Jed felt himself getting short of breath and his neck getting hot. *Lord, help me not to say just anything.*

"Well, Superstition Mountain isn't exactly on the common way home."

"And Ginny isn't exactly a common girl."

"Yeah, well . . . we agree on that, T.J." Jed stopped himself from saying more. "Anyway, forget it. Is that why you called?"

"Not really. Listen, we really need somebody like you to try out for the football team. I'm serious. The coach is hurting for someone to play defensive back. I think you have just the strength and speed for the spot. How about it?"

"Football's not my sport."

"It's a lot of fun, Jed. Hey, you don't want to spend the season sitting on the sidelines, listening to them cheer for somebody else, do you?"

"No, T.J., I don't want to sit on the bench listening to them cheer for someone else. I'm just not interested in the whole subject. OK?"

"Sure . . . OK. Listen, do you want to go to the Arizona State game on Saturday? They're playing U.S.C., and I've got some good tickets."

"I've got to work Saturday," Jed replied.

"Yeah . . . sure. Well, give me a call when you've decided to be friends again."

Jed didn't say anything to T.J. for the rest of the week. He hardly had a conversation with Catherine, and he didn't speak much to Ginny until Friday during chemistry lab.

"Well, we're supposed to inventory everything at our station. What do you suppose this is?" Ginny held a spiraling glass straw towards Jed.

"Ginny, let's go for a picnic up in the mountains tomorrow. We need to talk."

"I thought you had to work tomorrow." She tossed her hair back away from her green, penetrating eyes.

"Who told you that?"

"Well, T.J. said. . . ."

"T.J.?"

Ginny sighed in disgust and turned her head away from Jed.

"T.J. called and invited me to go to an Arizona State game with him tomorrow. He told me he had wanted you to go but you turned him down."

"But you didn't turn him down," Jed complained.

"Why should I? Do you want to ask Mrs. Johnson for a new lab partner?"

Jed stammered, then responded, "Uh . . . no. Not really."

"Me either." Ginny dug in the drawer for other objects. "Listen, I said 'yes' to T.J. because no one else asked me to go anywhere this weekend. You would hardly talk to me all week."

"I didn't have anything to say. I mean, all week I've wanted to talk, but I've been afraid I'd just blurt out something dumb like I did on Sunday. So I was trying to get by without saying anything."

"Did it work?"

"Did you list these? Eight of these beakers and a rack." He shoved them back into the drawer and pulled out another object. "No, it didn't work. I had a lousy week!"

"Me too." Ginny recorded each entry with her meticulous handwriting.

"You did?" Jed sat up and stared over at Ginny.

"Yeah. Don't look so happy. Jed, I like to have friends. Some of my friends are boys. But, well, you and me . . . we are kind of like special friends, and I've missed talking to you. I mean, you act like a jerk sometimes, but I still have missed being with you. We're sort of two-of-a-kind, you know? I just feel real comfortable around you. It's different with T.J. or the others. Does that make sense? Look at this thing." She held up a silver instrument. "It looks like something a dentist would use to inflict pain. Jed, why do you get so jealous?"

Jed didn't give Ginny an answer.

He didn't have one.

"Listen, if I say something right now it would be stupid and I'd regret it . . . but I do know what you mean. Can we talk tonight?"

"Sure, give me a call. Do you think we'll ever get this figured out?"

Jed sighed, "The relationship?"

"No," Ginny laughed, "this equipment inventory. What do you think we will use these earplugs for?"

"Don't ask." Jed took a big breath and relaxed. For the first time in a week he felt a glimmer of hope.

There is no one, I mean no one, cuter than Ginny Greenly when she smiles.

Right before dinner, Catherine barged into Jed's room.

"Big brother, I've got an awesome favor to ask. And you're the only one in the world who can help me."

Jed pulled off his headphones.

"Listen," Catherine continued, "remember when I went over to Ginny's and talked to her dad? Well, I need that kind of help."

"Who's dad do you want me to talk to?" Jed laughed.

"Ours!"

"Dad? About what?"

"He's just got to let me go with Brad tonight," she pleaded.

"But you've been pestering him all week."

"Please, Jed . . . go talk to him. He doesn't understand. I need someone to be on my side. I need to be with Brad. He's the only one who will listen to me."

"Catherine . . . you just can't control every situation in life. I ought to know."

"Jed!" Tears streamed from her brown eyes. "Please!"

"I'll go talk to him, but you know he won't change his mind."

Five minutes later Jed knocked on his sister's door. "Hey, Cath, can I come in?"

"Sure . . . what did he say?"

"He said 'no' you can't go. I'm sorry. But he did say you could invite Brad over for dinner after church on Sunday."

"Jed, I can't do that. I mean, I don't even know if Brad goes to church."

"You haven't talked to him about his faith?"

"See, I thought we might get to that tonight."

"Well, invite him to church with you Sunday. That's one way to bring up the subject."

"If I cancel out tonight, he'll never go anywhere with me again. Jed, you understand, don't you? There are some things you just have to do."

"I know that sometimes when I've thought that, I've been wrong," he cautioned. "Where are you going?"

"Tell Mom I'm going to Ginny Rinaldi's house."

"You tell her. Why the scarf?"

"So my hair won't blow."

"Walking to Ginny's house?"

"Yeah, walking to Ginny's house." Catherine tromped toward the back door.

"Catherine! Hey, be careful. . . . Don't do something dumb. You're my favorite sister," Jed called.

"Don't worry, big brother. If I ever get in a jam, I'll call you."

Jed yanked a package of cookies from the kitchen shelf and grabbed the telephone. He opened a cookie and licked the filling as he dialed. He heard Ginny's familiar voice.

"Hi, it's me."

"Hi, Jed. I'm glad you called. There's something I wanted to tell you."

"Really?" Jed flopped down on the kitchen floor and leaned against the wall. "I need to talk to you too."

"Yeah, well go ahead," she encouraged.

"You first," he probed.

"No, go ahead," she insisted.

"OK, but remember, sometimes my words come out all wrong. Listen, I'm really scared, and I do dumb things when I get scared."

"What do you mean—scared?"

"Well, I've been working for months to, you know, get settled in Arizona. You and T.J. have been really good friends. Then, all of a sudden, last weekend it sort of dawned on me that all of that was tentative, and I didn't really have any control over those relationships. I mean, we really might not be friends forever. You know. . . ."

"Is that what scared you?"

"Yeah. The part about having all the circumstances around me outside of my control."

"I guess that's where we have to trust the Lord, huh?"

"Yeah, that's exactly what I finally figured out. I'm sort of a faithful follower as long as I get to make all the decisions. Well, I made a decision today. Ginny, I really need you for a friend. There are just some things we can talk about that I can't talk about with anyone else."

"I know what you mean."

Jed sat up and replied, "You do?"

"Yeah, I sort of need a good friend like you too."

"Listen, Ginny, hang in there with me. I know I'll say some stupid things again. But I just get, you know . . . jealous of our . . . friendship."

"That's it? I mean, you only get jealous of the friendship?" Ginny pushed for more of an answer.

Jed took a big deep breath. "Ginny, I get jealous because you're the cutest girl I've ever seen in my life, and someday the Lord's going to cause you to fall in love with me and we're going to get married and buy a house with a pool and a tennis court out in Paradise Valley and raise three kids and own a big dog named Randolph."

There was a long pause on the phone.

"Ginny? Ginny? Did I really say that? Oh, man, tell me I didn't say that. I was being dumb again, wasn't I?"

Ginny answered with a soft, quiet voice, "Yeah."

"Sorry."

"Don't let it happen again."

"I won't."

"Jed."

"Yeah, Ginny?"

"It sounded good."

"It did?"

"Yes . . . except I want to live in Sedona, have four kids, and a small dog."

"Hey, no problem. I'm flexible." Jed couldn't remember having a greater time in his life than at this very moment. "Ginny, you had something you wanted to tell me?"

"Yeah, well, I called T.J. and told him that I didn't want to go to the Arizona State game tomorrow."

"You did? No fooling? You really did?"

"And I told him he ought to call you and ask you again. You two would have a great time."

"Call me? But I told him I couldn't. . . ."

"Yeah, I know. Well, I thought you might have had a change in plans."

"I don't know. But Ginny, thanks for not going. It kind of helps my weak trust, you know? I'm learning, really."

"Hey, T.J. isn't the only one I turned down this weekend. There's this new guy in school from California. His name is Brad something or other and he drives this nice looking Camaro. Well, he asked me out tonight."

"Brad asked you out?"

"Yeah, but I said, 'No.' He's kind of slimey."

"He's what?"

"Slimey. You know . . . the type that doesn't bother taking time to build a friendship. You know . . . a one-track mind."

Jed sank back down to the floor.

"But . . . Catherine . . ." he mumbled.

"Catherine what?"

"I think Catherine snuck out with Slimey. What am I going to do?"

"Trust the Lord and pray real hard."

"Yeah, yeah, yeah—but what am I really going to do? Ginny, don't you see . . . Catherine thinks this guy is . . . you're right, it would be a good place to start, wouldn't it?"

"You can't be in control of everything, Jed."

"It's a good thing . . . my record isn't all that great," Jed sighed as he grabbed two cookies and crammed them into his mouth.

Solid Gold

"Jed, this is the most horrible thing that has ever happened in my entire life!" Catherine sobbed.

"You need to see it from their point of view." Jed grabbed a green shirt out of the closet, and continued the conversation with his sister. "For starters, you disobeyed, lied, showed disrespect for your parents, acted irresponsible and put yourself in the possibility of harm. . . ."

"Oh, Jed!" Catherine moaned. "Did you ever get grounded for a month just for sneaking down to Pearl's Drive-In?"

"Uh . . . no." Jed pulled off the green shirt and searched through his closet for a different one to wear.

"For a week?"

"Nope."

"Jed, did you ever get grounded at all?"

He snapped up the sleeves on a tan western shirt, plucked up his comb and turned toward the mirror above the dresser. "Er, actually . . . no."

Catherine waved her arms in the air. "See? They're not treating me fair!"

"Catherine, just between you and me, this guy Brad doesn't sound all that great."

She flopped down on his bed with her upper lip starting to curl. "Says who?"

"Look . . . any guy that wants you to disobey your parents, well, it doesn't seem very smart."

"Brad needs me."

Jed tossed his comb on his dresser and got down on his hands and knees rummaging under his bed. "Needs you?" he questioned.

"Yeah, you know, to be his . . . you know . . . girlfriend. He told me he needs me."

Retrieving his grey cowboy boot, he sat down next to his sister and pulled them on. "Catherine . . . every time, and I mean every time, I've tried to hurry a relationship I've ruined it. There's no reason for you to act as dumb as I am."

"But Jed, this is different. . . . Jed?"

Jed was halfway down the hall.

Yeah, sure. It's always different. How come when you're a teen it takes three years before your brain catches up with the rest of your body?

For the next four weeks Catherine either pouted in her room or gabbed on the phone to Ginny Rinaldi. Meanwhile, Jed plowed into a heavy class load at school and put in as many hours at the Botanical Gardens as they would let him.

He did manage to find time for Ginny Greenly.

"Nine hundred bucks to fix my transmission!" Jed wailed. He shoved his Arizona State baseball cap to the back of his head.

"How much have you saved so far?" Ginny handed Jed one of her french fries.

He plunged it into the catsup before popping it into his mouth. "I've only got one hundred and sixty in the bank. Man, it will be March or April before I have my own wheels again."

"Yeah," Ginny sighed, pushing her sunglasses back up over the red bandana in her hair, "but look at me. I don't get my own car until I go to college."

"But that's different."

"Oh, sure . . . I'm a girl. I don't need a car, right?"

Jed grabbed up his milk shake. "Well, it's just. . . ."

"So I have to wait around for some guy with a cute smile to give me a ride?" she kidded.

He noticed that Ginny's green eyes always sparkled when she was excited. He leaned against the back wall of Pearl's and bounced his long legs up on the seat cushion. "Nah. You don't have to wait for him. . . . I'll give you a ride anytime you need it," Jed laughed.

"You *are* the guy with the cute smile, you jerk." Ginny bounced a french fry off Jed's cheek.

"Never start a food fight with a guy holding a milk shake." He faked dumping the contents on her hair.

"That's what I like about you, Jed," Ginny laughed. "You always act really mature."

"That's me—the epitome of etiquette."

"Well, Mr. nice guy, have you talked to T.J. lately?"

Jed sat up and pulled his cap down a bit, suddenly staring out the window at the parking lot. "Oh . . . yeah . . . sure. We talked yesterday."

"Did you really talk? I haven't seen you together much."

"Hey, I've been busy at work."

"Yeah, well, I wish you'd get it straightened out because I like visiting with T.J., but this puts me in an awkward spot."

When he turned back to look at Ginny, she was staring right into his eyes.

"So I didn't have time to go to a football game with him."

Raising her eyebrow, she continued the sentence, " . . . or go out for the football team . . . or work on a homecoming float . . . or. . . ."

Jed slumped back down into the booth at Pearl's Drive-In and spoke with almost a whisper, "or go with him to New Mexico."

Ginny sat up. "He invited you to go to New Mexico?"

"Actually, Mr. Bell called me up. He and T.J. are going over to check out that old gold claim."

"But you've been dying to go over there."

"I've got to work and save my money. Anyway, I don't know if T.J. really wants me to go."

"T.J. wants you to go," Ginny insisted. "His Dad wants you to go. . . . I want you to go!"

"How do you know T.J. wants me to go?"

"Jed! Don't start. . . ."

He flipped up his hands in resignation. "You're right. I need to go. Of course, I don't know if my folks would let me. They've been kind of strict since Catherine got grounded."

"Your parents said it was all right," Ginny encouraged.

"They what? You've talked to my folks?"

"Yeah. And your dad said you've been working too hard and need a break."

"You're not trying to get rid of me this weekend, are you?"

"Of course I am. Look, you've been tense for a month. It shows up in your eyes. And when you're tense, you don't smile very much, and I happen to think you have one of the two greatest smiles in Arizona."

"Two greatest? Who's the other guy?"

Ginny stood up, stretched, and searched through the crowded drive-in. Then she sat back down. "Oh, I haven't met him yet, but there's always a possibility."

This time Jed tossed a french fry at Ginny.

Mr. Bell flew the plane to New Mexico, with T.J. sitting in the copilot's seat. Jed looked on from the row behind. The air was clear and the ride smooth, yet he felt uneasy.

Ginny wants me gone. My parents want me gone. T.J. and I need to have it out. What in the world am I doing at 12,000 feet, flying to some old gold claim?

After a smooth landing at Las Cruces airport, two men met the plane and immediately pulled Mr. Bell aside.

T.J. tossed down the sleeping bags. "Jed, do you remember the last time you flew into Las Cruces?"

"Yeah, it was when your dad was missing. Kind of scary, wasn't it?"

"Yep." T.J. climbed down to the runway as Mr. Bell hussled over to the boys. "Look, they say I've got to fly to Farmington and check out some drilling rig. Can you two go on and examine the claim by yourself?"

"Yeah, sure, Dad." T.J. pulled off his beat-up, straw cowboy hat and scratched his head.

Mr. Bell helped the boys carry their gear over to a waiting Jeep. "You have a map. You can't wander too far before you hit the fence."

"The fence?" Jed asked.

"The one the government put around the range."

"The range?"

"You know, the White Sands Missile Testing Range."

"White Sands! Where they test the nuclear bombs?" Jed shouted.

"Hey, that was years ago. Besides, the fence keeps a person from getting in the wrong area," T.J. laughed.

It only took T.J. and Jed about thirty minutes to run out of paved highway and start bouncing down a dusty desert trail.

"How far is it?" Jed hollered above the grind of the motor.

"About sixty miles," T.J. shouted back. "The road's not too good from here on."

"Road? What road?" Jed challenged.

The noise, dust, boulders and potholes made conversation almost impossible. Jed spent the time gazing at the barren landscape.

Why would anyone in his right mind think that there was gold out here? This is God's left-over earth still in its raw form.

The minutes added up—one by dirty, gritty one—until two hours had passed.

"Look for a green post at a dry creekbed," T.J. called out to Jed as he folded the map and crammed it back into his pocket. They drove another three miles and then T.J. stomped on the brakes.

"This looks like it! Where's the green post?"

Jed stood up and stared over the windshield. "There's a creek bed, but I don't see any post."

"Yeah, well, I know this is the place. There will be a little grove of trees on the north side of the mountain."

Jed sat back down. "We haven't seen a tree since Las Cruces."

"Trust me." T.J. put the Jeep in four-wheel drive. They rolled, bounced and jerked their way up the streambed.

By the time they reached the clump of trees, the streambed had played out. They had to blaze their own trail.

"Man, we are going where no man has ever gone before!" Jed blustered.

The boys spent the next hour setting up the camp that would be home for the weekend.

"You ready to dig for gold?" T.J. asked.

"Yeah, I guess. What are we supposed to do?"

"Well, Dad and I found a few traces of color down in that little wash that we drove up. But those flecks of gold had to be attached to something more substantial. Let's lay out a grid, dig down to bedrock, then knock off and label some samples."

There was no shade where the boys worked and both of them soon found themselves ringing wet with sweat. After grubbing out ten samples, they headed back to camp.

"T.J., I don't understand why we are up here doing this? I mean, your dad could send in a team of engineers, bulldozers, heavy equipment, and strip this mountain down in no time."

"That's the problem," T.J. explained. "We're so close to the missile range that if they thought this was being developed, they would come in and claim it under public domain. As long as it's just a couple of guys, they'll leave us alone." T.J. gulped a big swig out of the canteen and handed it to Jed.

They climbed past the trees to the top of the mountain and sat down on some rocks facing west.

Suddenly, T.J. jumped to his feet and spun around waving his arms. "When I'm up here I feel like I'm on top of the world."

Jed stared toward the setting sun. "Man, you can see for hundreds of miles."

"I always figured this was the kind of place where God would go if He wanted some privacy."

Jed nodded. "Yeah, either here or the Grand Canyon. A lot has happened since we took that trip last year."

"We've changed some, I guess," T.J. added.

Jed took a big deep breath. "Not all the changes have been good, have they?"

"Yeah, I know what you mean." T.J. leaned back on a rock. "Sometimes I wonder if it was the best thing for me to stay in Phoenix and attend Northwest High. We were better friends when I was at the academy."

Jed plucked up a small rock and skipped it down the mountainside. "But that isn't your fault. Sometimes . . . well, the more you get to know people, the more you find things that bug you. I think that's why brothers and sisters have such a hard time getting along. I mean, you get to know all the details and then forget what a person's really like."

T.J. continued to stare off at the sunset. "Yeah. I'm getting tired of keeping up this image."

"What?" Jed stood on the rock next to T.J.

"Look, admit it. Sometimes I come across kind of . . . you know . . . arrogant," T.J. stated.

Jed climbed to a higher rock. "Yeah . . . rich, arrogant, talented, smart—*and* a lady-killer."

"See, that's the point! Everybody expects me to act that way, and I guess I get so carried away trying to please, I forget to be myself. Jed, I envy you more than any guy at school."

"Me? You envy me?"

"Man, you have a family . . . mom, sister, and a dad who has time to do things with you. You've gone out and done things on your own, like buying your own car. I don't know, it's . . . integrity . . . genuineness, I guess."

"You're putting me on, right?"

T.J. sat up and looked at Jed. "Nah. Ginny was right. She turned me down for a date. She said, 'Jed's my guy. He's solid. I know I can count on him!' "

"Ginny said that?"

"Yeah. Having friends you can count on, that's what it's all about, right?"

"Well, I'm happy just being Jed. I'd make a lousy second-string T.J. My car is never going to be new. I'll never be as tall as you are. I'll never have a bank account like yours. I'll never live in a palace up on Camelback—and I'll never be *the* quarterback on the football team."

"And you'll probably never sit in the middle of a crowded high school cafeteria and have it dawn on you that there is not one person on earth who knows what you are really like."

Jed stood silent as he thought about T.J.'s words. Finally, he stood up. "Hey, I'll concentrate on being Jed, and you specialize in being T.J. Let's get back on the same team."

"You got it, partner!" T.J. slapped Jed on the back.

The boys spent the next morning digging and gathering more samples. Most of the morning they worked shirtless, letting the New Mexico sun increase their tans. By 2:00 they had packed up their gear, loaded their samples and bounced down the mountain to the highway headed for Las Cruces.

T.J.'s dad met them at the airport and they gave all the ore samples to one of his assistants for processing.

"Jed, can you help Dad load up . . . er . . . I've got to make a phone call," T.J. called as he ran back toward the air terminal.

A few minutes later he returned.

Jed could tell that T.J. looked worried.

"Important call, huh?" Jed quizzed.

"Yeah . . . well . . . now, don't take this wrong, but . . . look, Jed, you need to call home right now," T.J. stammered.

"What? Call home? Call my folks? Right now? Who did you talk to?"

T.J. shifted his weight back and forth, "Look, I just called Ginny and she said. . . ."

"You called my Ginny?" Jed demanded.

"Listen, we've worked that through, right?" T.J. cautioned. "There was something I had to talk to her about . . . just as friends. Anyway, she said your folks are frantic because Catherine ran away from home today with some guy named Brad."

"You're kidding! Catherine wouldn't do something that dumb."

Jed started toward the terminal, then turned back. "T.J., listen . . . you can call Ginny anytime, really."

T.J. threw his arm around Jed's shoulder. "Go find out about Catherine. I think of her as my sister too."

"Well, don't tell her that." Jed spun back around, and then turned back a second time. "T.J., if she took off, I'm going to go find her."

"I know."

"And I'll need you to help me."

"You can count on that!" T.J. hollered.

Jed raced to the public telephones. It was the first time in his life he could remember being so worried about his sister.

Lord, please don't let anything bad happen to her!

The Search

Jed Rivers shoved open the airplane door and leaped down the stairs to the runway. He didn't stop running until he met Ginny Greenly inside the air terminal.

"Where's my folks? Did they find Catherine? Is she all right? What about . . . this Brad?" Jed grabbed his side and struggled to catch his breath.

Ginny slipped her hand into his and pulled him along toward the front entrance parking lot. "Listen, your parents are out looking for Catherine, so they wanted me to pick you up. She took off right after Sunday school, but your folks didn't notice her missing until after church."

"And good old Brad . . . he's with her?" Jed yanked open the air terminal door and the two of them caught a blast of hot Phoenix air.

"Yeah . . . we think so. Anyway, Brad's not at home either."

"How about his parents?"

Ginny pulled Jed across the loading zone, dodging hotel busses. "Who knows? Brad's mom is on a cruise, and his dad lives in California."

Jed paused, gazing across the crammed parking lot.

"Hey, royal couple, wait up!"

127

Ginny and Jed whipped around to see T.J. jogging through traffic, carrying his bags and Jed's.

"Royal couple?" Ginny still held tightly to Jed's hand.

T.J. threw his arm around Jed's shoulder. "Yeah. I looked over here and said, 'They are going to be North West High's next homecoming king and queen.'"

"Not hardly. They usually pick seniors." Ginny tugged on Jed's arm, pulling both guys along.

"Texas Jack Bell predicts you'll be easily elected. What's the news on Catherine?"

"Nobody's seen her. Man, I'm really worried," Jed openly admitted.

"Texas Jack? T.J. stands for Texas Jack?" Ginny pressed.

"Eh, yeah . . . sure. Jed's told you that before, hasn't he?" T.J. scratched the back of his head. "Listen, let's drive around town and see if anyone's seen Catherine."

Ginny pushed the boys through a crowded row of cars. "Jed, how come you never told me about T.J.'s name?"

"Because good friends can keep secrets. Listen, what car did you bring down here?" He searched the lot for the Greenly's station wagon.

"Oh, here it is." Ginny pointed to a blue Mustang. "Nice car, huh?"

"My Mustang!" Jed dropped Ginny's hand and hurried to the car. "How did you drive it to the airport?"

Ginny and T.J. walked up slowly. "It's no big deal," she added, "especially after the Hansen Garage rebuilt the transmission." She handed Jed the keys.

"What? You had the transmission rebuilt while I was in New Mexico?"

"Yeah, we wanted to surprise you."

"We?" Jed opened the door and T.J. crawled into the back seat.

"Me and T.J." Ginny continued. "We couldn't bear to see this car sitting in the driveway all year, so we chipped in our money and had it fixed. You owe each of us $441.23, payable by June first."

Jed scooted his bucket seat forward. "I don't believe this. How did you guys pull this off?"

Ginny pulled her sunglasses down.

"That's why you wanted me to leave town?"

"And that's why I called Ginny from New Mexico," T.J. broke in. "I wanted to make sure it was ready."

Man, I still can't believe you guys really did this!" Jed started up his car and steered it out of the parking lot. "I mean, nobody ever . . . you know . . . I never even thought. It's incredible. This is incredible!"

"Hey," Ginny punched Jed in the arm, "good friends can keep secrets, right T.J.?"

Jed turned the car off the freeway and headed west on Van Buren Street. "I suppose my folks have checked at Pearl's, and the shopping mall, and Ginny Rinaldi's house," he mumbled.

"Yeah. And they checked all the hospitals, police stations, and movie theaters," Ginny added. "Right now they are visiting, personally, each one of Catherine's friends to see if they have a clue."

"How long has she been gone?"

"I guess about seven hours now."

"Ginny, where would she go?" Jed turned the car up Central Avenue and drove slowly as they entered the downtown area.

"Well, they sure wouldn't come down here," Ginny said. "I mean, by now they could be in Tucson or Flagstaff."

"Or Yuma, Palm Springs, or Mexico!" T.J. called out from the back seat.

"Ginny, if you were a super-romantic freshman . . . crazy enough to run away . . . where would you want to go?" Jed asked.

"The Cactus Flower Resort," Ginny shot back.

"Whew! Scottsdale! Top of the line." T.J. exclaimed.

Jed turned right on McDowell Road. "I've never heard her mention that."

T.J. added, "It costs five hundred bucks a day."

Jed scanned the sidewalk as they stopped at a red light. "It's a cinch they didn't go there."

"Well, you asked me where I'd want to go, and that's what popped into my head. Did Catherine ever mention any luxurious location like that?"

Jed cruised across the intersection, then slammed on his brakes and pulled over to the curb. "The Pines!" he shouted.

"In Prescott?" Ginny added.

"Yeah. Since it opened last spring she's wanted to stay at The Pines. She read this deal in the paper about the Governor's Suite and decided that's where she wanted to go."

Ginny looked at Jed. "Should we call them and check it out?"

"Wait," T.J. interrupted. "I don't want to discourage you or anything, but I know all those places—and frankly, I just don't think old Brad has that kind of money. I think we're going about this wrong. We're trying to figure out what Catherine's thinking. But what about this guy, Brad? Where would *he* want to go?"

"I don't even know him," Jed shrugged.

T.J. leaned forward between the bucket seats. "Let me take a wild guess. If I were some slime ball picking up young girls, I think I'd go over to Treasure Cove, or someplace like that."

"In Tempe?" Ginny probed.

"But isn't that just a cheap motel?" Jed complained.

"Why else would a guy run off with a freshman girl?" T.J. avoided looking either Ginny or Jed in the eyes.

"T.J.," Jed pulled back onto the street, "I hope you are wrong . . . man, I hope you are really wrong."

"Me too," T.J.'s voice softened, "me too."

The trio pulled into the outer parking lot at Treasure Cove about 7:30 p.m., but they couldn't locate the brown Camaro. Next they tried the Palm Garden Luxury Inn, the Desert Oasis Manor, and the Blue Pelican Palace.

"Hey, this is going nowhere," Jed finally admitted. "I've got to call home."

"Yeah. Find a phone booth and see if your folks have had any . . . luck." The last word seemed stuck in Ginny's throat as she spoke it. "Jed, maybe we should pray about this?"

Without slowing his car, Jed began, "God . . . we're really worried about Catherine, and to tell you the truth, Lord, we don't know what to do. She's really young, and she doesn't always . . . you know." Jed was silent for a moment. "Don't let her get hurt, Lord. Please help us find her before she messes up her life something bad. In Jesus' name."

"Hey look!" T.J. interrupted, "a phone booth."

"Jed signaled, then crossed the street and pulled into a closed service station, parking next to the public telephone.

He was out of his car and digging in his pocket for change when he noticed that the receiver had been ripped off. He slammed his fist against the glass.

"Great! That's just great!" In anger, he spun around facing the busy traffic of the street.

"T.J.! Is that a brown Camaro? Look, over at the stoplight. Isn't that Brad's car?" Jed leaped into his Mustang, slammed the door, and tore out onto the street.

"Jed, take it easy. You'll rip up this new transmission," Ginny cautioned.

The brown car was two blocks away but Jed swerved around a slow moving truck and floored the accelerator. By the next stoplight, he caught up with the Camaro and pulled along the driver's side. He shoved his car into neutral, yanked back on the emergency brake, and jumped out of the Mustang on a run. With a clenched fist, he banged on the window of the Camaro.

Brad Herndon rolled his window down a couple of inches and peeked out at Jed. Brad's hair and shirt were soaking wet.

"Where's Catherine!" Jed yelled.

"She's . . . she's not in here." Brad glanced up nervously at the red light signal.

Jed stooped down to look in the car.

"Where is she?" he demanded.

"I don't know," Brad whined. People on the sidewalk began to stare at them.

"What do you mean, you don't know? She's been with you all day, right?" Jed continued yelling.

"Yeah . . . yeah, but we had this, er . . . argument . . . and she took off." Brad started to pull his car through the intersection, but T.J. shot out of the Mustang and stood in the crosswalk, blocking it.

"Come on, you guys, the light changed," Brad pleaded.

"Took off?" Jed was still screaming. "Took off where? Where did you last see her?"

"Down near the zoo, at the bridge. She got mad and tromped off into the riverbed."

Shouting voices and angry horns blared at Jed.

"And you left her there? Brad, you're the biggest jerk I've ever met. Don't you. . . ."

Suddenly Brad turned the steering wheel hard to the right and shot around T.J. The whole flow of traffic flooded past Jed.

He and T.J. climbed back into the Mustang and tried to follow the Camaro, but Jed knew it was a lost cause. At the next intersection Jed maneuvered a U-turn and headed back south.

"Where are we going?" Ginny finally asked.

"To the riverbed."

"But she could be out there anywhere," Ginny added.

Jed turned left at the next corner and spoke without emotion, "I'll find her . . . I'll find her."

Just off Washington Street, he turned down a dirt levy. For fifteen minutes they bounced down the dusty maintenance road in silence. Without warning, Jed slammed on the brakes so hard that the engine stalled. He stood straight up on the seat and braced himself against the windshield. Shading his eyes from the glare of city lights, he shouted, "Hey . . . that's her! That's Catherine!"

Within seconds, all three were out of the car and straining to look through the evening glare.

"Where is she?" Ginny yelled.

"Look! Down there! Across the riverbank. See those scrubby cottonwoods? There's a girl walking, carrying something on her back!"

T.J. bounded up to the top of a cement barrier for a better view. "Are you sure? Jed, it's almost dark. I can hardly see across the riverbed."

"It's her, I know it. It's the way she walks when she's pouting, or. . . ."

Ginny held on to Jed's arm. "Or what?"

"Or hurt." Jed climbed up to where T.J. stood. "Catherine!" he yelled, cupping his hands around his mouth. The grind of a semi-truck on the street behind him silenced his next attempt. "Look, I'm going down there. Meet me with the car at the Seventh Street bridge."

T.J. slid down the sandy bank of the Salt River behind Jed, leaving Ginny with the Mustang.

"Jed, wait!" T.J. grabbed Jed's arm. "Hey! Man, we can't go running up in the dark screaming at some girl. I mean, if it's not Catherine . . . we might be arrested or something."

"Don't slow me down T.J., it's Catherine." Jed pulled free and ran through the loose sand. He had lost sight of the girl in the evening shadows. Finally, he stopped and leaned over at the waist, trying to suck in more air.

His shoes were full of river sand, his side was cramping. He listened in the dark as he heard T.J. stop alongside of him. Both boys were gasping for a breath.

The desert sky was clear and one star could already be seen in the north. Jed wiped a grimey hand across his sweating forehead. In frustration, he screamed at the top of his voice, "Catherine!"

Only the distant noise of a busy, surrounding city responded to his yell.

He brushed again at the mixture of sweat and tears on his face, took a deep breath and yelled, "Catherine Marie Rivers!"

For a moment, it was absolutely quiet in the riverbed. It was as if Jed's shout cleared the air of all sound. Neither he, nor T.J., moved. Then he heard footsteps in the blurred shadows ahead of him.

"Jed?" The voice sounded on the verge of tears. "Jed? Is that you?"

Chills shot right up Jed's arms and down his back.

"Cath? Catherine!"

In the darkness Jed saw a figure emerge, throw down a duffel bag, and run to him. She grabbed him around the neck, and he held her around the waist.

Neither Jed nor T.J. said a word as they listened to Catherine's sobs.

Jed couldn't remember any time in his life when he had been of comfort to his sister. There was always Mom or Dad or Grandma, or someone else to take care of Catherine. He didn't know what to do, so he patted her head and kept mumbling, "It's OK, now . . . it's OK."

It was T.J. who finally began to speak. "Cathy . . . are you hurt? I mean, do you want us to get you to a doctor, or police, or anything?"

Jed started to release his sister, but she held on tight.

"No . . . we didn't . . . do anything," Catherine gasped. "Honest, Jed, he never touched me." She held Jed even tighter. "I just feel like the stupidest kid in Phoenix. Jed, why can't I be smart like you are?"

135

It was a good five minutes before she regained her composure and began to loosen her grip on her brother.

"Come on, Cath, let's go home. Ginny's at the bridge with my car."

They started trudging through the sand, with T.J. following behind.

"How did you find me down here?"

"I don't know for sure. I mean, we were frantic—all over town—then I thought you might have gone up to The Pines. . . ."

"In Prescott?"

"Yeah, but T.J. . . . ."

"Why would you think I'd go there?"

"And then Ginny suggested that we ought to pray. But we still couldn't find you. Then we spotted a brown Camaro, and Brad said you were down along the river. . . . Maybe the Lord was just being good to us. What is all this, Cath? Did you really decide to run away?"

Catherine held on to Jed's arm as she walked. "Look, all of this sounds crazy. I mean, I can't believe it myself. It's just, you know, for awhile, Brad made me feel very grown-up and important—like there was one person on earth who couldn't live without me. I've never felt that way before. I didn't want that feeling to stop. So, well, Brad and I decided to run away to Texas."

"Texas?" T.J. piped in.

"He's got an aunt in El Paso, and we were going to stay with her. Anyway, we spent most of the day down at South Mountain Park, talking. . . . I think we were trying to justify what we were doing."

"Then he told me he had a place lined up for us to spend the night, and we'd leave for Texas tomorrow. Well, his great plan was for us to stay at the El Matador Motel. Jed, when I saw that horrible green building with the paint peeling off the door, I almost threw up. I just knew this whole thing was crazy. I kept saying to myself, 'What am I doing here? The Lord doesn't want me here! I don't want to be here!'"

Jed helped his sister scale the steep riverbank. "How did you get away from him?"

"Oh, Brad's not completely rotten. I just told him the whole thing was wrong, grabbed my duffel bag, and ran down to the river."

"Why the riverbed?"

"Because I didn't want him to follow me and talk me out of leaving." Catherine brushed the tears from her eyes on the sleeve of her blouse.

"How did you know he wouldn't follow you down here?"

"Oh, well . . . I did throw his car keys into the motel swimming pool." She broke into half a smile. "I guess I did one thing right."

"Keys!" Jed shouted as the trio climbed over the cement barrier onto the Seventh Street sidewalk. "I told Ginny to meet us around here, and then ran off with the keys in my pocket! We've got to walk all the way back to. . . ."

"I don't think so. Look!" T.J. motioned at the blue Mustang parked on the far side of the street.

"Ginny?" Jed called as they crossed the pavement. "Hey, I've got the keys. How did you get the car started?"

"Catherine! Are you alright?"

The two girls embraced with sobs.

"Yeah, my big brother found me," she confessed.

"Ginny, how did you get my car around here?"

"I hot-wired it. No big deal."

Suddenly, Catherine blurted out, "I'm stupid. Dumb. And ugly. A real airhead. And the only date I've ever had was with some jerk. I think I'll move to the Grand Canyon and live in a cave the rest of my life."

"You what? You hot-wired my car?" Jed insisted.

Ginny still hugged Catherine. "It's tough being fourteen."

"It's the pits." Catherine climbed into the back seat of the blue Mustang as Jed tossed the duffel bag into the trunk. T.J. slid in next to Catherine.

"You can't hot-wire my car, it's got this device that. . . ."

"Oh, Jed, relax . . . I stuck a finger-nail clipper handle into the key slot and the motor cranked up. That's all. We'd better call your folks."

Catherine lowered her head. "Oh, man, I bet they're really mad at me."

Jed started up the car and flipped a U-turn, traveling toward downtown.

"They're probably more scared than mad right now," Ginny added.

"Yeah, the mad will start as soon as they know you're safe," Jed cautioned. "Ginny, did you really hot-wire my car?"

"I bet I'm grounded for a whole year," Catherine offered.

"You kind of deserve it, right?" Jed nodded.

He could see Catherine in the rear view mirror as she stared out at the city lights. Tears trickled down her cheeks. "Yeah, I know," she said softly.

Jed pulled into a service station and sprinted to the pay phone. T.J. hussled toward the soft drink machine as the girls headed for the ladies' room. The boys were standing beside the car when they returned.

"What did Mom and Dad say?" Catherine asked.

"Well, they had just gotten back to the house. Dad asked if you were safe, and Mom cried. They want us to hurry home."

"Yeah, I'll bet." Catherine slunk down into the back seat and sat silently as they drove north on Central.

They hit a red stoplight on Indian School Road, right in front of Pearl's Drive-In. Catherine leaned forward. "Jed, do you think I'm pretty? And don't you lie to me!"

He turned to look at her. "Listen, Cath . . . when you were only five, and had that white dress with the red bows—I thought you were the cutest little sister on earth. Then, when you were nine and had the braids, and rode the pony at the parade down in Akron, I told Barry Reilley that I had the sharpest looking sister in town. And I can tell you one thing, someday you are going to be one beautiful woman."

"Yeah, but that's not the point. Right now . . . at fourteen. Do you think I'm pretty?" she repeated.

Suddenly Jed shifted the car into neutral, jumped out into the street, and pulled Catherine out of the back seat.

"Jed!" she protested.

He yelled at the top of his voice toward all the guys sitting on their cars over in front of Pearl's, "Hey, you guys! I'm Jed Rivers and I want you to know that my sister Catherine is one of the three cutest girls in the whole state of Arizona!"

139

He pushed the blushing Catherine back into the car and they zoomed across the intersection when the light changed.

"Jed! That's the most embarrassing, humiliating, disgusting . . . the nicest thing anyone has ever done for me," Catherine blurted out. "And if I start crying again, I'm going to clobber you."

Then she turned to Ginny and T.J., "You know, I've got one great brother."

"And I've got one great best friend," T.J. added.

"Yeah, and I've got one great question," Ginny insisted. "What do you mean 'one of the three cutest girls in Arizona?' "

Jed laughed, "Well, there's Cath . . . and you . . . and. . . ."

"Yeah? Go on, hotshot . . . who else?"

Jed stuck his head out the car window and scanned the girls walking along the sidewalk. "Hey, I'm just leaving my options open."

"Oh, no, you're not!" Ginny leaned over to hold onto Jed's arm . . . and kissed him on the cheek.

Back to the Bible is a nonprofit ministry dedicated to Bible teaching, evangelism and edification of Christians worldwide.

If you have any questions about how you may know God personally, please write to us:

> BACK TO THE BIBLE
> Youth Department
> P.O. Box 82808
> Lincoln, NE 68501